Signs of the Savior

Signs of the SAVIOR

Ralph L. Murray

BROADMAN PRESS,
Nashville, Tennessee

4281-32

ISBN: 0-8054-8132-X

Dewey Decimal Classification: 226.5

Subject heading: BIBLE. N. T. JOHN

Library of Congress Catalog Card Number: 76-44038

Printed in the United States of America

DEDICATION

To our grandchildren

MILLICENT AND MATTHEW

neither of whom is old enough to read
this book, but both of whom have
brought new joy and wonder to the lives of
their grandmother and grandfather;

and

To their parents,
our son Joe and his wife Sue

Contents

For the Reader

What prompts a person to write a book? Answers to that question will be as varied as books and writers. Therefore I cannot answer for all books or all writers; only this book and this writer.

This book began with a request that I write Bible study materials on John 1—12 for one of our curriculum series. When I had completed that task, I still felt that my work was unfinished. The detailed study material had been done, sifted, and some of it set down on paper. But it was didactic. The purpose had dictated the style, and the style had less vitality than I liked. I felt a need to mold that background study into inspirational material, which is, after all, a preacher's native air. Moved by that need I proposed to Broadman Press an inspirational book on John 1—12. The result you hold in your hand.

Why John 1—12? Well, John's Gospel divides itself into two parts—the Book of Signs (2—12) and the Book of Glory (13—20). This division is John the writer's own design. In that last half (13—20) John views Jesus' passion, crucifixion, and resurrection as part of the ascension to glory. That ascension is finally accomplished in Jesus' return to the Father in glory. The geometric design of God's in-flesh self-disclosure could be the parabola. John 13—20 is the upside of that geometric figure.

The downside of that figure begins in the prologue

(1:1–18). From the prologue John passes directly to Jesus' public life and ministry. In John's account of Jesus' public life and work we catch a glimpse of the inscrutable God. For John, Jesus' miracles were not wonders or powers, but signs—signs of the Savior. They tell us who Jesus really is.

Seven of those signs make up the Book of Signs, but each is interwoven with narrative. The sorting-out process of sign and narrative has divided interpreters of the Gospel, since not all are agreed on which is which. In this book the signs are identified as follows:

1. Jesus turns water to wine at the wedding in Cana, with subsequent events which end with another wedding (2:1 to 3:36).
2. Jesus heals the Gentile official's son (4:46–54).
3. Jesus heals the lame man (5:2–9).
4. Jesus feeds the five thousand (6:4–14).
5. Jesus exerts power over nature (6:16–21).
6. Jesus gives sight to a blind man (9:1–41).
7. Jesus raises Lazarus (11:1–53).

These are John's signs of the Savior. Interspersed in this book are chapters based on the narrative that links the signs together, as well as chapters based on the signs themselves. Taken together, John 1—12 provides a vein a little book like this can probe but never exhaust. I hope it helps you.

RALPH L. MURRAY

1 To Begin With
John 1:1–18

Sometime ago William Manchester wrote a book about the assassination of President Kennedy. He called his book *The Death of a President.* One of the more serious charges against the book is that the material does not present an unbiased account of tragic history, but rather a highly partisan interpretation of selected facts. Manchester, so the criticism goes, does not serve history nearly so well as he serves himself.

As one who has written a bit myself, I must confess an admiration for Manchester's literary style. It is brilliant. His approach to well-known facts is imaginative, even though controversial. He has given the reading public a very intimate and readable account of the death of President Kennedy, though it may reflect his own affectionate bias toward the late president. If he has not done the service intended, still I—for one—would not say he has done us a disservice.

I suppose it was this book that sparked a very interesting thought—at least to me. Imagine that in the first century someone had undertaken to write a book giving us the detailed account of the death of Jesus. What would it have been called? *The Death of the Nazarene?* or would it have been *The Death of God?*

And then I began to imagine the different turns the book might have taken. Had a Stoic written it, probably the death of Jesus would have been seen as unswerving loyalty to truth as Jesus was given to see it. An Epicurean, on the other hand, would have painted Jesus as taking himself and his world too seriously. An Essene would doubtless have condemned Jesus for getting so involved in the lives and affairs of the world. A Pharisee would have interpreted our Lord as a self-serving opportunist, insisting that he wanted to be a law unto himself.

It was at about this place in my train of thought that the thing you have already thought of dawned on me: we do have such accounts. Four of them as a matter of fact. We call them Gospels. One was written by a social outcast, a publican. His name was Matthew. Another was authored by the son of well-to-do Jews who had come under the liberating influence of the larger world of the dispersion. His name was Mark. Another biography was drawn together by an accomplished man wholly outside the Jewish tradition. He was a Gentile physician by the name of Luke. And one other such account was written, this one by a Jew of disarming sophistication, considering that he was a fisherman early in his life. This last writer was John.

And very interesting is the fact that each of these writers saw Jesus a little differently. For Matthew, Jesus was the fulfillment of Jewish expectations. For Mark, Jesus was the Lord of man and of nature. Luke saw Jesus in the human setting and emphasized family more than any other. John, probably the last to write, presented Jesus in an urbane, philosophical vein, interpreting Jesus in a novel and wonderful way as the answer to the fundamental questions of our existence.

The basic questions of John's world were very much the same as our own. They had to do with an understanding of God: what God is like; an understanding of the world: what

God has to do with it; and an understanding of ourselves. There were many different sets of answers that have been worked out to these questions, but John wrote as a Christian. Note what I just said: a Christian. John wrote, not just as one who believed in God, but as one who believed that God has made himself known in Jesus Christ. John took no pains to hide this particular bias. As a matter of fact, toward the end of his work, he came right out and stated his purpose plainly: "These are written, that ye might believe that Jesus is the Christ, the Son of God; and that believing ye might have life through his name" (20:31).

So when we read the Gospel of John, we recognize that we are exposing ourselves to a biased witness. This is not just history; it is an interpretation. It is—first and last—a frank witness about a way of looking at life, of experiencing life. It is presented (as the author plainly stated) to bring others to such a commitment. This is an ancient William Manchester, on an elevated level, whose subject is "The Death of the Nazarene."

We shall confine our attention in this chapter to the first eighteen verses, sometimes called the prologue of John's Gospel. It is John's opening statement. In these verses he set the tone for all that would follow. And in them we have three profoundly helpful affirmations. These are the heart of his Gospel. This is the good news. You will find the truths openly stated. John is frankly direct. And those truths lie quietly as a foundation for all that he is going to say. Could I name the truths? First, God is good. Then, God has not abandoned us. And this last, we may know God, and the life of God in us through faith in his Son.

God Is Good

One of the popular ideas of John's time was that there

had to be at least two gods. One was a good God; the other a bad god. And temporarily, at least, the bad god had gotten the upper hand. That was the explanation given for all the pain, anguish, and tears common to man. Man was himself in the grips of this bad god. Not only man, but his world as well. It was all the messed-up product of an evil god.

To such an idea John adroitly addressed himself by the subtle use of a literary form. In a bit we shall see how he identifies the God who made this world and us with a good God by his use of a literary form. But right here, we look at the symbolism John employed—darkness and light.

The Gnostics used to explain that between Genesis 1:1 and 1:2 the evil god took over, and darkness reigned. From there on, every delightful and good thing is counterfeit. It only has the appearance of goodness. It is a trick of the evil god. It is really evil and is meant to deceive us.

John confronts this set of answers head-on. He starts out with the good God of Genesis 1:1, and then places alongside him the Logos—the Word. And then without even taking a breath, he says everything that was made was made by this good God through the Logos. In the King James Version, verse 5 reads, "And the darkness comprehended it not." If we take that old English word to mean "surround" or "hold in seige," then we get the idea intended. John is saying the darkness never did overcome the light. Never.

This is John's way of saying, "If things look dark for you, don't concoct some god to blame it on. You have turned from the light and lost your way. But God has come into this darkness of yours to lead you back to the light. That is just how good God is."

Now if we can believe that God is good, that God will not

cook up some caprice or mischief, then we have a base on which to build. Then, even in adversity, we can assume a *good purpose.* We can take Romans 8:28 at face value, "Moreover, we know that to those who love God, who are called according to his plan, everything that happens fits into a pattern of good" [1] (Phillips). God may not have sent your adversity. It could very well be your own foolishness. But God will *use* it. God is capable of no mischief. God is good.

We have the word of Jesus for that: "If ye then, being evil, know how to give good gifts unto your children, how much more shall your Father which is in heaven give good things to them that ask him?" (Matt. 7:11). That is where John starts: God is good.

God Has Not Abandoned Us

The art of the writer comes through when you take a close look at his opening statement. The first three words of his treatise are the same words with which the Old Testament Scripture opens: "In the beginning. . . ." This is John's way of saying that he will address himself to the same questions addressed by the first chapters of Genesis.

And what were they? Genesis sets before us a loving and eternal Father who makes a garden called Paradise. In that garden of perfect delight he placed his darling, man. Man has one responsibility—he is to have all this, *under* God. But man's instinct is toward insubordination. His drive is to rearrange the framework of responsibility to suit himself. He is ungrateful to his Maker. He strikes out on his own, with a style all his own. This basic decision is followed by a growing avalanche of deceit, lies, murder, and social as well as inner chaos. Man thoroughly smashes the good intentions of a good God.

Now John goes back to the earliest dawn of creation and takes a frank look at man's irrational preference of darkness and chaos. But where the Old Testament finally gives man a law to live by, John goes further. He says God has given us more than a law; he has given us a Savior.

In Genesis, God made a garden, gave man a law, and withdrew. In John, God comes back into the garden with man and stoops to help him put back together the broken pieces.

The Jews believed that God came to men through the Torah—the Law. This was God's Word. It had come to them through Moses and the prophets. But this belief had a deadening effect. God was always cast in the molds of the past. Malachi lamented a lost reverence for God and his altar (Mal. 2:7), but it is understandable. God was the God of the dead; but what about the living?

To the Jews with their exalted reverence for the Law, John bears his witness: "God has another Word. It is Jesus, the Nazarene, who has pitched his tent among us, and who is full of grace and truth" (see v. 14). This is a way of saying, "God has not abandoned us. He has come to pitch his tent with us even as he tabernacled with his people in the wilderness. God has wrapped up the intent of his Law in a Person."

This was hard to understand; even harder to believe. The Jews, for the most part, rejected it. Others tried to explain it. They said Jesus only "seemed" to be one of us. He could not be both God and man. Still others put it another way. He was a man, they said, whom God adopted at his baptism in a special way. And so the discussion ranged.

But John answers: "The Word became flesh, and dwelt among us, full of grace and truth" (v. 14, RSV). John's reasoning may have gone something like this: "Just as man cannot think without symbols by which to express his thoughts, so God's disclosure of himself to himself requires a means of communication. That means can be called the *Logos*.

"The Logos, which is God's means of self-disclosure within himself, is also his means of self-disclosure outside himself. In God's self-disclosure to man, the Logos became flesh. The divine Logos, which did not diminish God's divinity, by participation in the world through the flesh, was able to make divinity known to men."

Whatever John's thought, he said it succinctly, and in his own way, "The Word became flesh and dwelt among us, full of grace and truth."

Truth is *what* God gave men in Jesus. Here is the answer to man's questions about the fundamental mysteries of his existence. Would man know life in its fullness? Look to the life of Jesus. Would he know how to meet death? Look at the death of Jesus. Would he know of the hope beyond the grave? Look at the resurrection of Jesus. This is God's truth. Its circles inscribe all the significant questions of man.

Grace describes *how* God sent it. It was not that we deserved it; not that we had it coming to us. It was that God, in his goodness, loves us. In spite of ourselves, he loves us. While we are yet enemies, he loves us. Though we are helpless, he loves us. God has not abandoned us. He has come into the shambles we have made of his garden, and into our dark despair, to help us recover a lost glory. That is the meaning of this man, Jesus. That is the Gospel's interpretation.

We Can Know God for Ourselves

We can have his life in us through faith in his Son. I can

imagine someone saying about now: This is all very nice, but how does it help me pick up the tab of stress, sin, and anxiety in my daily life? That is where the water strikes the wheel for me.

Ah! How right you are! And John faces this for us squarely. Let him state it for himself: "But as many as received him, to them gave he power to become the sons of God, even to them that believe on his name: which were born, not of blood, nor of the will of the flesh, nor of the will of man, but of God" (1:12–13).

If I were to put in steps the means by which we can make this grand truth our own, it would be something like this:

First, each of us must adopt a working hypothesis that centers in God. God is a loving Father, who is concerned for me. As I grope in the darkness of my own irrational, self-defeating apathy or rebellion, he comes to me. He has expressed his concern in a supreme act of self-giving in Jesus Christ. Christ comes into the world of history, and by his Spirit into my own inner history, to relieve me of my guilt and estrangement. He comes to assure me of my place with the Father, in spite of all that I have done or not done.

Second, I must act on this assumption. For me this would mean an open profession of faith in Christ as Savior, baptism, and identification with Christ through the church. It would mean that every day I would seek to live out the full implications of this commitment in my work, my play, my leisure, my reading—the full scope of my life. In a word, this action means that God in Christ becomes the very center for me. He is the integrating hub of all my interests, all my concerns. It is love for him that motivates me, that gives a particular style to my life.

Isn't this Christ at the center of things what most of us are missing? Does this not explain our lackluster lives? Our sense of guilt? of apathy? of uncertainty? Our being at loose ends?

John made his witness. But it was with Christ at center. And if your experience of Christ is not as intense, not as satisfying, perhaps you need to look at yourself rather than him. For there is evidence that Christ can come in as much fullness, as much power as he ever did, if we will receive him.

Sometime ago a Rumanian, Pastor Richard Wurmbrand, was witnessing before the Judiciary Committee of the United States Senate. He was telling of the Communists' brutality and murder of Rumanian Christians. The particular incident I relate here is given simply to support the claim of John that when Christ is the center, we have God's power and God's life in us.

> And now a Sunday morning political officer of the prison comes, the whole brigade is gathered, and just at random he sees a young man. He calls him, "What is your name?" He says the name. "What are you by profession?" He said, "A priest." And then mocking the Communist said, "Do you still believe in God?"
>
> This priest knew that if he says yes, this is the last day of his life. We all looked at him. For a few seconds he was silent. Then his face began to shine and then he opened his mouth and with a very humble but with a very decided voice he said, "Mr. Lieutenant, when I became a priest I knew that during church history thousands of Christians and priests have been killed for their faith, and notwithstanding I became a Christian and I became a priest. I knew what I became. And as often as I entered the altar clad in this beautiful ornate which priests wear I promised to God, 'If I will wear the uniform of a prisoner, then also I will serve him. Mr. Lieutenant, prison is not an argument against religion. I love Christ from all my heart.' "[2]

And then Pastor Wurmbrand added:

> I am sad that I can't give the intonation with which he said these words. I think that Juliet when she spoke about Romeo, she spoke like that. We were ashamed because we—we believed in Christ. This man loved Christ as a bride loves the bridegroom.[3]

Later on, the man who gave this testimony, and bore the marks of the Lord Jesus in his own body, was given special police protection because of the danger in which his own commitment to Christ had placed him.

John was a man like that. His is a biased witness. His witness bears the bias of experience, of the new beginning of life which is in Jesus Christ.

2 People Who Need People
John 1:35–42

Barbra Streisand has sung in a hauntingly beautiful song that people who need people are the luckiest people in the world.[1] Perhaps one reason her recording of that song has such powerful appeal for many people is that they recognize in it the basic truth that relationships are terribly important.

Andrew, about whom John wrote in our Scripture passage, apparently was the kind of person who liked people. The few times we come upon him in the New Testament he is in the middle of doing something nice for someone else. For examples see John 12:22, or 6:8–9, or our text—1:40–42. They illustrate that quality in Andrew.

Come to think of it, because Andrew liked people, others were helped and blessed. Among those who were helped because of his liking for people is Simon Peter, Andrew's own brother. Perhaps we would do well to pause briefly and measure this brother of Andrew, who owed his relationship to Jesus to his brother's influence. To know about Simon Peter is to know the importance of Andrew.

Simon Peter strides across almost every page of the Gospels; he centers in nearly every action. There are 171 references to Simon Peter in the New Testament, and each of the Gospel writers heads his list of the apostles with Simon Peter's name. One of the primary sources of the written gospel is—in all probability—the remembered gospel of Simon Peter as set down by John Mark after Peter's death in Rome. Making every allowance, we are left with the apparent fact that Simon Peter was the first among equals.

Moreover, he was the natural leader of the Christians in the first, fluid days following Jesus' ascension. He is the human explanation of the vitality and invincibility of the early church. Post-ascension Christianity in Jerusalem cannot be explained apart from the leadership given it by Simon Peter.

So it is right that we devote a chapter to Andrew and his recruitment of his brother Simon to Jesus' movement. We will follow the unfolding events, first in Andrew's introduction of Jesus to Peter, then in Jesus' call to Peter for discipleship. Finally, in the larger dimension Jesus brought to the life of Simon Peter, we will find the full fruit of Andrew's witness.

Introduction to Jesus

John tells us that one of the first apostles to meet Jesus was Andrew, Simon Peter's brother. We do not have the full story; it is told with dots and dashes. But if we can piece together what we have, we may conclude that Andrew met Jesus, not in Galilee, but in Judea. Perhaps Andrew had gone to Jerusalem to visit the Temple. Once there, he found the city buzzing with talk of a desert preacher called the Baptizer, who was preaching in the Jordan River valley. To hear him might mean a delay of a day or more, but Andrew decided it was worth it, and he detoured to the Jordan Valley on the return trip. It was that very day that Jesus appeared before John, asking for baptism. It was there Andrew first saw Jesus.

When Andrew returned to Galilee, the first thing he did

was go directly to Simon his brother and tell him about Jesus.[2] What he said we cannot know in full. John disclosed that Andrew shared his thrilling discovery that Jesus was the Messiah. Just what that meant to Andrew or to Peter, we can only surmise. It is safe to venture they both had much to learn.

But we must not miss this important fact: Simon was introduced to Jesus by his own brother. This is essential Christianity. No ecclesiastical machinery in the world can compare for one moment with the value, with the effect, of that personal touch. Person to person, heart to heart, friend to friend—that is the way the earliest Christians learned about Jesus. We have never found a way to improve on that.

One of the cherished memories in my own family is the conversion of my father's youngest brother. As a boy I can remember my father's concern for Uncle Lee. I recall one summer evening, after discussion and prayer, making a special visit with my father to Uncle Lee's home. My father went, with his Bible in hand, to talk to his younger brother about becoming a Christian. I was too young to have a part in that conversation but not too young to know the purpose of the visit. While I played out in the yard with my cousins, my father talked to his brother and his brother's wife about becoming Christians.

That witness did not bring forth immediate fruit. It was a few weeks later, on a Sunday evening, that our telephone rang about 10 o'clock. In a gospel service, in another church than ours, Uncle Lee and his wife had made public their profession of faith.

Years ago now, Dad died. A heart attack took him out. And then just a few months after, Uncle Lee died of leukemia. Through all the years after that eventful Sunday night Uncle Lee and his family were faithful Christians. When the news came of Uncle Lee's death, I remembered one of the last times I had seen him. It was at my own father's funeral. There was that quiet Christian faith undergirding his own sorrow, but I sensed that my uncle was suffering the loss of more than a brother; he had lost a friend—the friend that introduced him to Jesus.

When I wrote a note to my uncle's widow and her family, I referred to this boyhood memory, and then continued: "In a sense it is a wonderful thing that Dad went first. When Uncle Lee came to the heavenly portals, I am sure Dad was there to meet him, and as he had once before, he took him and brought him to Jesus."

It was Andrew, Simon's brother, who first introduced him to Jesus. Isn't there someone near and dear to you that you need to introduce to Jesus? The old spiritual speaks to our need:

> If you cannot sing like angels,
> If you cannot preach like Paul,
> You can tell the lost of Jesus—
> You can say He died for all.

The Call to Discipleship

If we can reconstruct the events of those momentous days, then it must have been sometime after Andrew's first contact with Jesus—after the temptation in the wilderness, and the imprisonment of the Baptizer—that Jesus came into Galilee.

And we must go carefully now. We could miss the background events of the story. It is all told in terse, telegraphic style, and we thread our way cautiously.

It may have been John who was with Andrew the day they first heard this strange preacher called the Baptizer, down there in Judea. The preaching of the Baptizer had strangely stirred them. He was a bold, blunt man who called the shots just as he saw them. Even then, it seemed likely that he might be headed for trouble.

Luke summarized the preaching of John, and the least we can say of it is that John had every segment of society in his sights. He called the Pharisees, who were proud of their racial and cultural heritage, a "generation of vipers." For the publicans, the Baptizer had a sharp word. But his choicest excoriation was reserved for the high jinks of the family of Herod the Great. (See Luke 3:1–20.)

Now Herod the Great had been a much-married man. He had one son by Mariamne, who was a daughter of the famous Maccabee family of priests. His name was Herod Philip. He lived as a private citizen with his wife Herodias in Rome. And Herodias was the daughter of her husband's half-brother, Aristobulus. One day Herod Antipas, another son of Herod the Great by still another wife, came to Rome for a visit with his half-brother Philip and Herodias. (Now Herodias was also the niece of Antipas!) Well, Herod Antipas was so taken with the charms of Herodias that he seduced her, persuaded her to leave his half-brother Philip, and come back to Jerusalem as his own consort. So here was the governor of Judea living with his sister-in-law and his niece (all the same person), and compounding his misdeed by having betrayed the hospitality of his own brother.

And the Baptizer had some choice words for the Herods. For the notice he took, John landed in the dread desert dungeon Machaerus, and later lost his life.

Mark and Luke tell us that after John went to prison, Jesus came to Galilee.

All these events were in the background. Although Peter

had never heard the Baptizer preach, he knew the essential theme as reported by his brother Andrew. He also knew of Jesus and the strange words the Baptizer had spoken about him as the Lamb of God. So when Jesus appeared on the lakeshore one morning while Peter was busy arranging his nets for the day's work, Peter was knocked completely off balance. Andrew had already taken up with Jesus. The message he preached—like that of John—was of repentance and belief. Suddenly Peter asked himself, "What difference does my religion really make? If I were to discard the whole business, would I be any different?" Essentially, Simon was confronted with the fact that there was no dynamic, positive transfer from his religious beliefs into his everyday life.

"What difference *does* my religion really make?" That is a good question. We might well pause and ask it of ourselves. Or we could put it another way: What is the use of my life? If I were to sum my life up in one word, what would it be?

George Bernard Shaw found such a word for his life one day. It was the word *foolish.* He stood one day at a mammoth rally in Queen's Hall in London to celebrate the Armistice after World War I. Led by a massive choir and a great organ, the audience sang, "O God, Our Help in Ages Past," the Isaac Watts hymn which is almost the religious national anthem of English-speaking people. As the volume of voices blended and swept over Shaw, he was deeply stirred. The words, which actually paraphrase the Ninetieth Psalm, sing of the eternity of God and the fleeting tide of man's years. They seemed to cast up the question of meaning for the whole of Shaw's life and its work.

A pastor standing nearby looked out of the corner of his eye and saw that Shaw was deeply moved. He remembered a page in one of Shaw's books in which he made a kind of inventory of his soul, which included, he said, "a cathedral." At the end of the hymn, as they sat down, Shaw whispered, "Doctor, I would rather have written that one hymn than all my foolish plays." [3]

And what is your word? the word that sums up all your life? A strong impulse in us all propels us to run from the full blast of life. That there is tragedy in greatness, pain in pleasure, darkness in light, ugliness in beauty, death in life—this is hard to accept. In fact, we do not easily accept it. Like the ostrich, we tend to hide our heads in the sand. Or like the trapped fox, we gnaw at our own paws. Or like the rabbit, we run.

Well, that morning, as the clear-eyed Realist stood before him, Peter decided it was time to quit running. He wanted a better word than foolish for the sum of his life. He came face to face with the fact, as our fathers used to say, that "he had a hell to shun and a soul to save."

Andrew had sown the seed; now it was harvest time. Because of Andrew, Simon was prepared for Jesus' challenge: "Come, follow me."

The Larger Dimension

So Simon Peter, the brother of Andrew, made his first tentative response. He left his nets, his boats, his business; he began the new adventure.

Some of us tend to think—all unconsciously—that Jesus' call to Simon was a call to the ministry, or something like that. But it was not. It developed into a full-time vocation for Simon, but it would not have had to. The call was to discipleship. This world needs doctors, dentists, lawyers, merchants, mechanics, clerks, typists, teachers, nurses, salesmen, mothers, fathers—faithful disciples in all walks of life. The Christian vocation means essentially that you make your vocation, whatever it is, a glory to Christ.

You have doubtless heard the story of the baker in the monastery who, unlike so many of the others there, had never taken on monastic orders. "What do you do for the glory of Christ?" asked a visiting abbot. "I bake," came the reply. "No," countered the abbot, "what is your Christian vocation?" "I bake," replied the peasant, "to the glory of Christ."

It was this sense of the Christian vocation within the vocation that explains the vitality of Christianity in the first century. Dr. Goodspeed reminds us:

> We must remember that most of the missionary work of the first generation or two was quietly done, personally and often incidentally, by busy men and women who had believed and communicated the gospel to the people they knew or encountered as they went about the ancient world for whatever reason. Only thus can we explain its early appearance in Damascus; that was why Saul was sent there by the high priest; and its presence in Rome, in surprising strength . . . significant enough to call forth Paul's letter to the Romans by A.D. 56, though he had never been there.[4]

We started this chapter with a reference to Streisand's popular recording, "People Who Need People." The comment was made that Andrew was such a person, and he was. He loved people; he loved Jesus even more. His love of Jesus impelled him to share with his brother Simon a marvelous discovery: "We have found the Messiah." As a result, Simon became Peter, first among equals and a leader of the early Judean church.

People who need people are lucky, so the song says. Well, people who love people enough to share Jesus with them are more than lucky. They are good stewards of God's grace and may enjoy the kind of good fortune Andrew did.

What would the world be without Andrews?

3 Come and See

John 1:43–46

Belief is important. It is the structure, the framework, and the spring of action. Dr. W. L. Jarvis of Australia illustrates that for us. He tells the story of a trip he took to the Fiji Islands. A native Fijian who was acting as guide did the unusual by asking the tourists if they were Christians. One tourist was impatient and wanted to get on with the sightseeing. The guide said, "But I'm a Christian, and I want to know about you." The impatient tourist wanted to know what difference that made. Soon they came to a spot which the guide described as having native historical significance. To the impatient man the guide said: "Do you see that pot? My ancestors used to cook white men in that pot and eat them. Were it not for Christianity, I might be eating you instead of guiding you." [1]

Belief is important.

But beyond the structure of ideas and the contour of concepts is experience. It is not enough to recite a creed. Nor to be baptized. Nor to take communion. These are experiences which flow from one central experience, and that experience gives all else its meaning.

Perhaps I can throw light on this truth with a story from the life of Walt Whitman. He went one day to a planetarium to hear a very learned astronomer lecture on the heavenly bodies. And to use his own lines, this is what happened:

When I heard the learn'd astronomer;
When the proofs, the figures, were ranged in columns before me;
When I was shown the charts and diagrams, to add, divide and measure them;
When I, sitting, heard the astronomer, where he lectured with much applause in the lecture room,
How soon, unaccountable, I became sick and tired;
Till rising and gliding out, I wander'd off by myself,
In the mystical moist night-air, and from time to time,
Look'd up in perfect silence at the stars.[2]

That's it! And that kind of experience is exactly what happened to Nathaniel. Philip had been caught by the magnetic Christ, and he did the most natural thing in the world. He went to a friend, Nathaniel, and said, "We have found him, of whom Moses in the law, and the prophets did write, Jesus of Nazareth, the son of Joseph."

But Nathaniel was skeptical. Too many had been singled out with premature enthusiasm as the Christ. And Nathaniel asked one question which was calculated to throw a damper on Philip's enthusiasm, and to make him take a sober look at the facts in the light of common day: "Can *any* good thing come out of Nazareth?"

But Philip knew that no amount of argument would convince his friend. Very wisely, he put his challenge in three small words: "Come and see."

There is profound wisdom in such an approach. In fact, in matters of faith and intuition, there is no other approach. In this chapter I want to make three observations designed to suggest that the only way any of us will come to know Jesus is to do just what Nathaniel did: "Go and see!"

The Paralysis of Analysis

Though Christianity must have its theologians and its apologists, there is a deadly danger in mere intellectual exercise about faith. The apostle Paul warned the Corinthians, "Though I have all knowledge, and understand all mysteries, and have not love, it profits me nothing." The experience of Christ is a personal experience, beginning with commitment and growing from that commitment into every part of life.

You remember the limerick about the centipede?

> The centipede was happy quite
>   Until a toad in fun
> Said, "Pray, which leg goes after which?"
> That worked her mind to such a pitch,
> She lay distracted in a ditch,
> Considering how to run.

Thought is important, but it is irrelevant unless it finds its roots in the facts of experience.

When Igor Sikorsky was a lad of twelve, his parents told him that competent authorities had already proved human flight impossible. Yet Sikorsky built the first helicopter. And in his American plant he posted this sign:

> According to recognized aerotechnical tests, the bumblebee cannot fly because of the shape and weight of his body in relation to the total wing area. The bumblebee doesn't know this, so he goes ahead and flies anyway.

Let me cite a couple more examples of how rational analysis, if followed, could have impaired progress. In 1829 an Ohio school board refused to permit a debate in the schoolhouse on the question, Are Railroads Practical? They said that if God had designed his intelligent creatures to travel at the frightful speed of fifteen miles an hour by steam, he would have foretold it by his prophets. And Bishop Milton Wright of the Methodist Church once proclaimed on a public platform that any man who claimed he could fly was guilty of an ignorant blasphemy. But in 1907 at Kitty Hawk, North Carolina, two young men did fly.

Their names were Wilbur and Orville Wright, sons of that Methodist bishop!

The point is this: analysis without experience can lead to paralysis. All experience, including Christian experience, begins at this point: "Come and see!"

Believing Is Acting: *Come* and See!

Philip invited Nathaniel to act. That was wise, for the essence of believing is acting. Do you remember the childhood story of the boy who cried, "Wolf! Wolf!"? He made that cry so often that the villagers ceased to believe. And then when the wolf really came down on him, the boy cried, "Wolf! Wolf!" but the villagers went complacently about their business. They did not act because they did not believe the boy's cry.

Search the pages of the New Testament and see if you can find a miracle that does not involve some action. And in the opposite direction, you have the absence of action in Nazareth as told by Mark in chapter 6:

> He went away from there and came to his own country; and his disciples followed him. And on the sabbath he began to teach in the synagogue; and many who heard him were astonished, saying, "Where did this man get all this? What is the wisdom given to him? What mighty works are wrought by his hands! Is not this the carpenter, the son of Mary and brother of James and Joses and Judas and Simon, and are not his sisters here with us?" And they took offense at him. And Jesus said to them, "A prophet is not without honor, except in his own country, and among his own kin, and in his own house" (vv. 1–4, RSV).

Here was Jesus, who had done so many mighty and wonderful works, powerless. Why? Because there was no willingness to take the first step; to "come and see." If we will take one step in our darkness toward Christ, he will advance a mile toward us in blazing light.

Believing is acting. "Come and see."

Believing Is Seeing: Come and *See*

Once Nathaniel acted, he came eventually to believe. That end is a likely result of action. If you will stop to ponder with me a moment, you will discover how. To begin with, we see with the physical eye. In that sense "seeing is believing."

But there is also another sense in which we see with the mind and the heart. And in that sense "believing is seeing." Once we have seen, then belief is further confirmed, and "believing is seeing" even more profoundly.

This process is behind all scientific experimentation. The scientist believes a certain thing to be true. We might call it an intuition. Scientists call it a hypothesis. So when Louis Pasteur proposed his hypothesis that disease is caused by a germ and that inoculation with an antitoxin will kill the germ and cure the disease, the doctors were skeptical. But Pasteur said to the scoffers, "Come and see!" and today we inoculate people with flu virus against flu.

In 1907 the German physicist Albert Einstein wrote down a little formula $E=mc^2$, and it was an invitation to the whole scientific world to "come and see." Thirty-five years, and thousands of man-hours and millions of dollars later, the Italian physicist, Enrico Fermi and his associates "saw." What they "saw" was nuclear fission.

So hypothesis is the scientist's way of saying what Philip said to Nathaniel: "Come—and you'll see!" And once you have seen, you believe more firmly than ever.

Now this is also true in the spiritual world. First you act, however tentatively. But you act. As Nathaniel did, so you must do. You go to "see" for yourself. That in itself admits the possibility of belief. And once you have begun, then you truly "see."

Harold Begbie has a book entitled *Twice-Born Men.* It is the story of some of the world's greatest men and their conversion. In the pages of that book you can read of Augustine, Francis of Assisi, Ignatius Loyola, Martin Luther, John Wesley, William Wilburforce, Toyohiko Kagawa. These are men who believed enough to begin the life of discipleship. And in the unfolding of life, they came to see, as Nathaniel did, that Jesus is indeed, the Son of God and the Savior of men.

One of the truly great men of our century was Albert Schweitzer. As a young man he was invited to become a member of the faculty of one of the great European universities as a teacher of philosophy. During those same years he became one of Europe's most renowned concert organists. At the age of twenty-five he decided to give the rest of his life in service to Christ, and acting on that decision, went back to study for a medical career. Upon graduation, Dr. Schweitzer went to Lambarene, French Africa, to give his life in humble service to the African people.

Of course, many thought Dr. Schweitzer mad. And in answer to their questions, Dr. Schweitzer wrote a book entitled *In Quest of the Historical Jesus.* In that book he throws out his own challenge to "come and see." Here it is:

> He comes to us as One unknown, as of old, by the lakeside, he came to those men who knew Him not. He speaks to us the same word, "Follow thou me!" and he sets us to the tasks he has to fulfill for our time. He commands. And to those who obey him, whether they be wise or simple, He will reveal Himself in the toils, the conflicts, the sufferings which they shall pass through in his fellowship, and as an ineffable mystery, they shall learn in their own experience Who He is.

Whatever your circumstance or question, I offer this simple proposition with respect to Jesus: "Come and see!"

Will you?

4 Joy in Jesus
John 2:1–11

There are several "signs" in John's book of signs—a subsection of his Gospel, found in chapters 2 through 12. These signs occur on the level of the senses but point beyond themselves to the transcendent—God in the midst of life. So we have the overtones of the eternal in the midst of time. Poets, who see the mystery of life more clearly than most of us, speak of such experiences. Elizabeth Browning put it this way:

> Earth's crammed with heaven,
> And every common bush afire with God;
> And only he who sees takes off his shoes—
> The rest sit round it and pluck blackberries.[1]

And Joseph Mary Plunkett saw his Lord in the familiar all about him:

> I see His blood upon the rose
> And in the stars the glory of His eyes,
> His body gleams amid eternal snows,
> His tears fall from the skies.
> I see His face in every flower;
> The thunder and the singing of the birds
> Are but His voice—and carven by His Power
> Rocks are His written words.
> All pathways by His feet are worn,
> His strong heart stirs the ever-beating sea,
> His crown of thorns is twined with every thorn,
> His cross is every tree.[2]

This may be too mystical for us, yet we must try to get into

John's way of looking at things. And this is his way. Ever since John met Jesus, the commonest experience was shot through with wonder. Heaven was eternally tapping him on the shoulder.

The first of John's signs took place at a wedding. The story is familiar—the turning of the water into wine. But the story is only a means, not an end. The literary unit of which the wedding of Cana is the introduction continues through to the end of chapter 3, where the unit concludes as it began—with reference to a wedding.

It must be noted that this is not a news report. John put his material together in sovereign disdain of sequence. Others had "set down in order" the events in the life of this Jesus. John interpreted him. To John the fundamental wonder of Jesus and those days they had together lay in the fact that this was the means God chose to disclose his true self to men. This was how the Word of God came to John, and now John would share that Word with his reader.

Our purpose here is to try to hold in view the framing of John's thought. In this first unit—the sign of the wine and the wedding—John was describing the essence of true Christianity. He began by saying it cannot be a barren, inadequate legalism. Even John the Baptist bore witness to that.

The unit then moves to Jerusalem and concludes with the long conversation of Jesus and Nicodemus (3:1–15). In that conversation John introduced the wholly new level of human existence possible: a life that is reborn; a life from above. This new life is as different as wine is different from water.

And John closed the unit with the theme that recurs in his book like a haunting melody: choosing and becoming. I make my choice—once Christ comes to me—and that choice in turn makes me.

Now could we look at these divisions of John's thought more carefully?

An Inadequate Legalism

Some notions die hard. Both the Pharisees and the disciples of John the Baptist clung to the notion that the law represented the best and the highest word God had ever given man. To this notion the Evangelist gave the *coup de grace* by telling the otherwise unreported story of the wedding in Cana.

You may remember the story (2:1–11). Jesus and his mother had been invited to a wedding in Cana of Galilee. At some point in the festivities, the mother of Jesus approached her son and asked him to relieve the embarrassment of the host. He had run out of wine. After some demurring, Jesus asked that six stone jars used for purification purposes and holding some twenty or thirty gallons apiece be filled to the brim with water. When the servants drew out of these jars for the guests, all exclaimed on the superior quality of the replenished supply of wine which had been drawn as water.

Now with an economy of detail, John moved through that story to make his point: "This, the first of his signs, Jesus did at Cana in Galilee, and manifested his glory; and his disciples believed in him" (2:11, RSV).

Clearly, the point of this story is the superiority over ordinary wine of the water turned to wine by the word of Jesus. Further, the six stone purification jars represent for John the law, the legalism of Judaism, and John the Baptizer.

What was it the law produced? Its *aim* was to produce a right relationship with God expressed in a right relationship with one another. The point of the whole Deuteronomic Code, even in its religious laws, was to produce a person of character, of sensitivity toward the needs of his fellowman. All the way through the Old Testament law, the ancient question, Am I my brother's keeper? seems to be answered with an insistent and resounding yes!

The *aim* of the law was to produce a person in right relationship with God and his brother. But what did the law produce?

In the eighth century B.C. Amos said the law had produced a man prolific in his religious devotions but insensitive and immoral in his relationships to others:

> "I hate, I despise your feasts,/and I take no delight in your solemn assemblies./Even though you offer me your burnt offerings and cereal offerings,/I will not accept them,/and the peace offerings of your fatted beasts/I will not look upon./Take away from me the noise of your songs;/to the melody of your harps I will not listen./But let justice roll down like waters,/and righteousness like an everflowing stream" (Amos 5:21–24, RSV).

For Amos, the law had produced a barren, immoral legalism. Micah, who preached in Jerusalem at about the same time, agreed:

> "With what shall I come before the Lord,/and bow myself before God on high?/Shall I come before him with burnt offerings,/with calves a year old?/Will the Lord be pleased with thousands of rams,/with ten thousands of rivers of oil?/Shall I give my first-born for my transgression,/the fruit of my body for the sin of my soul?"/He has showed you, O man, what is good;/and what does the Lord require of you/but to do justice, and to love kindness,/and to walk humbly with your God? (Mic. 6:6–8, RSV).

In the sixth century B.C., Jeremiah surveyed the ruins of Samaria and saw the storm-warnings flying for Jerusalem. He knew that it was the "inhumanity of man to man" that had brought down the mace of judgment. But where the law had failed as a written code, Jeremiah dreamed of a new day with an internalized code; what legalism had failed to produce, this new spiritual power would:

> "Behold, the days are coming, says the Lord, when I will make a new covenant with the house of Israel and the house of Judah, not like the covenant which I made with their fathers when I took them by the hand to bring them out of the land of Egypt, my covenant which they broke, though I was their husband, says the Lord. But this is the covenant which I will make with the house of Israel after those days, says the Lord: I will put my law within them, and I will write it upon their hearts; and I will be their God, and they shall be my people. And no longer shall each man teach his neighbor and each his brother, saying, 'Know the Lord,' for they shall all know me, from the least of them to the greatest, says the Lord; for I will forgive their iniquity, and I will remember their sin no more" (Jer. 31:31–34, RSV).

This barren, sterile legalism persisted in the fourth century, too. Malachi protested: "Have we not all one father? Has not one God created us? Why then are we faithless to one another, profaning the covenant of our fathers?" (2:10, RSV).

The law had failed. It produced a quality of life that was impoverished of feeling, of sensitivity toward one's own brother. And impoverishment in human relationships inevitably means an impoverishment of relationship between man and his Maker.

Which leads me to ask a very troubling question: What is it we are trying to produce in our churches? What is the concern in your own worship? If mere numbers is the goal, then whatever effectiveness we have means nothing. It is a barren institutionalism. It is the substitution of religion for integrity. Our goal should be to produce a people of compassion, responsibility, integrity, and concern. There is enough flat, tasteless, polluted moral water in the world; what the world is dying for need of is people whose lives have a different and distinctive flavor.

John began this discussion of the first sign by artfully portraying the barren inadequacy of mere legalism.

New Life from Above

A time-gap exists between the introductory sign and the further development of the theme. How much we cannot know for certain. At least time enough for Jesus to go from Galilee to Jerusalem, stopping enroute for a few days with his family in Capernaum.

And then, by means of a conversation, introduced by Jesus' cleansing of the Temple—a sure attention getter—John gave the antidote for barren legalism. It is the idea of taking the way of the cross as one's very own. I die that I might be born anew. I do not generate this kind of life; I receive it. I forget what may hurt me and begin to see what hurts my brother. I find God in making God's work in the world truly my own. In my openness to my brother, to his hurt and his need, I find God and my own true self.

Obviously, this goes against nature. How can I have strength for such a life? for such risks? I cast myself upon God. I open my life to him. I walk out into each new day, seeking to know what is God's good. Then, I give myself to it, asking the Father to give me of Christ's spirit. Nicodemus stands as the illustration.

Choosing and Becoming

Nicodemus was never the same after that nighttime conversation. Later on John artfully weaved into his story how Nicodemus opened himself to hurt; how he risked all his hard-won attainment by the symbolic act of claiming Jesus' body and giving it a proper burial. (We shall look at this in more detail in chapter 6.)

Christ came to Nicodemus, and Nicodemus chose—

hesitantly at first, but with gathering strength and courage—to follow in his way. Nicodemus chose, and look what he became: the one who gave the last tribute of affection and devotion to the human Jesus.

If you were to ask Nicodemus how he would want us to remember him: as a member of the Sanhedrin, as a "ruler of the Jews," or as a simple follower of Jesus, braving the hurt Jerusalem could inflict to bury the body of the Savior, we know what it would be. He would want us to remember him as he became because he followed Jesus.

John ended this first sign of the Savior with a wedding, even as he began it. He reported a conversation of John the Baptizer with some of his disciples. He spoke of Jesus as the bridegroom, and of his own joy in bringing the groom to the bride. And then we have this final word of the gospelist, tying it all together: "He who believes in the Son has eternal life; he who does not obey the Son shall not see life, but the wrath of God rests upon him" (John 3:36, RSV).

Where do you stand right now? Do you stand with Christ? Or do you stand to one side, avoiding the risk, the pain, the embarrassment? That may seem to be good to you now—to avoid the pain—but you run the risk of final loss. Choose Christ while you have time. That is the good. To defer, to delay—that is the evil. It leads to eternal night.

> Jesus is standing at your heart's door,
> Standing and knocking, He's knocked before.
> This is the question you face once more:
> What will you do with Jesus? [3]

5 Getting Rid of Bad Religion
John 2:13–23

In matters of monetary circulation, Sir Thomas Gresham, founder of the Royal Exchange in London, defined a tendency of men everywhere. He said that they tend to spend the worn, the thin, or the defaced coin in preference to the new, full, unmarked coin. This statement has been called Gresham's law, and may be stated something like this: Bad money has a tendency to drive good money out of circulation.

There is a kind of Gresham's law in religion. It could be stated succinctly: *Bad stuff drives out the good, since it is more easily understood and enjoyed.* Jesus ran into the operation of that law in the Temple on a visit there for a Passover Feast. What he did in response to the bad that he saw practiced there is the substance of the second part of John's first sign.

In the last chapter we took in the part of a literary unit developing this sign. It was the wine and the wedding. That, as well as this incident, are stage-dressing for the conversation of Jesus and Nicodemus which follows in John 3. Here we have one of the more subtle art forms—a sign within a sign. It is like a story within a story, or a plot within a plot, which all Shakespeare scholars have had to trace out under the watchful eye of some English teacher. So we must back up to catch this second part of the first sign.

We need to understand a little of that which incensed Jesus. It was the Passover time—something like our Christmas and Fourth of July all wrapped into one. A part of the Passover observance was to offer in the Temple a suitable sacrifice. And every self-respecting Jew aimed at least once in his life to observe Passover in the environs of Jerusalem and the magnificent Temple there.

But travel and ritualistic sacrifice animals were not too congenial. Most of the pilgrims arrived on the scene without a sacrifice animal. Those who had them discovered the animals had to pass the scrutiny of a rigid examination. The end result was that the Passover offered a built-in opportunity for the chief priest and his cohorts to engage in a little holy merchandising. Doves for the poor; lambs for the rich—and all at a nice markup. As if that weren't enough, every worshiper had to pay a Temple tax—in Temple coinage. By the time an uninitiated novice had finished his Passover observances, he was clean in more ways than one. The Temple establishment had a nice thing going for them, and the Passover profit alone has been estimated at somewhere between forty and fifty thousand dollars.

Yet, not many minded. We could not expect the priests to be offended by these arrangements, and they were not. But we might expect some of the worshipers to become incensed. There is no evidence of such. They took the graft as a part of the expense of convenience. So everybody involved—and each for his own reasons—had let the bad drive out the good in their religious observances.

When John related how Jesus stormed through the Temple area, overturning the tables of the moneychangers, releasing the doves and the lambs, John saw in it a "sign." And that is what we are looking at now—this sign in the cleansing of the Temple.

It seems to me the sign points to at least three things. First, it points to *something in ourselves*. Then, it points to *something in our Savior*. And then we shall see that it points to *something about our future*. Shall we take them in that order?

Something About Ourselves

Earlier I mentioned Gresham's law: Bad money has a tendency to drive the good money out of circulation. I also said there is a spiritual version of Gresham's law, and it is that spiritual version which Jesus protested. It is a part of the sign, and as such points to something in each of us. That something might be put this way: Each of us has a tendency to reduce our religion to its lowest common denominator.

We begin this reductionism with our beliefs. We want them to be neat, logically consistent, minimal in demand. It is too much bother to study the Bible—to go to the source. We would rather have somebody tell us what it says. And we want them to put its truth into catchy little slogans. The catchier the better, and never mind the fringes.

And we have them. Take one we of our particular demomination like, "Once saved, always saved." Now that is Calvinism, truth to tell, and it is not even original with us. But it scarcely does Calvin justice. Calvin did not start with the saved; he started with God. Calvin said God was the sovereign. And when kings were sitting on nearly every throne in Europe, everybody got the picture. God was king.

Then Calvin went on to say that man was subordinate to God in everything—even the salvation experience—just as a citizen was subject to his king. Being a rigorous logician, Calvin went on to define God's sovereignty as so irrevocable that once a person had experienced the crisis of conversion—even though it might be against his own will—there was nothing that could undo it. But Calvin had a lot of ifs and ands in his logic that the *hoi poloi* would not fool with, and when they had boiled it down to an irreducible minimum, it was simply: "Once saved, always saved."

The difficulty is that in the interest of economy not everything was said that should be said. That which was said is true enough, but it was simply not enough said. They should have added, "And being saved makes a difference in one's life-style."

That is simply to illustrate this reductionism I refer to.

The Jews in Jesus' day had reduced their religious obligations to a severe minimum: Keep a code of laws the best you could; make a once-in-a-lifetime pilgrimage to the Temple in Jerusalem; offer there a sacrifice. All the lacework that offended Jesus was embroidered on that minimal set of beliefs.

Once you reduce the beliefs to some kind of bare essential, you reduce the demand. This must be the explanation for our spiritual anemia in the churches. This sign tells us something about ourselves—the bad drives out the good. We settle for that which can be easily understood and enjoyed.

But such simple, even fraudulent, formulas produce the kind of commitment which can blithely ignore obvious—even crying—needs. An anonymous revision of an old hymn could well be our theme song:

> I'll go where you want me to go, dear Lord,
>   Real service is what I desire,
> I'll say what you want me to say, dear Lord—
>   But don't ask me to sing in the choir.
>
> I'll say what you want me to say, dear Lord,

I like to see things come to pass,
But don't ask me to teach girls and boys, dear Lord—
I'd rather just sit in my class.

I'll do what you want me to do, dear Lord,
I yearn for the Kingdom to thrive,
I'll give you my nickles and dimes, dear Lord—
But please don't ask me to tithe.

I'll go where you want me to go, dear Lord,
I'll say what you want me to say,
But I'm busy now with myself, dear Lord—
I'll help you on some other day.

Something About Our Savior

A second feature about this sign John gave us is that it points to something about our Savior. He did not go through the proper Temple authorities to secure a permit for his housecleaning. He just went to work.

Which is to say that Jesus is his own best credential. He does not *have* authority; he *is* authority. He comes because it is his right; because of what he is; because of who he is.

The judgment of our Lord fell like a mace upon the sham of a watered-down religion. It was not the worshipers Jesus drove before him. It was the faithless functionaries who either condoned or misled them. Jesus' judgment fell upon an unworthy worship, which in turn rested on bad theology. And he judged because he loved. He loved as God loves. Therefore he judged that malpractice of religion; he condemned what it produced; he excised those who were supporting it.

Which brings me as a minister of Christ's Word to address you with his presence. He comes now, as he came to them—in love and in judgment. How much of his demands have you trimmed away? Discipleship begins with a commitment to him as Savior and Lord. It continues with baptism and church membership. Very soon the follower of

Jesus has an irresistible impulse to give outlet to this new life in Christ through service. It is a life of witness and work. How far have you gone? Are you looking for more ways of serving, or less? More giving of self, or less?

Nels Ferre once wrote a provocative little book called *The Sun and the Umbrella.* It tells of a race of men who lived in a badly-lighted old barn. He called it the House of Legality, but you could call it just anything that corresponds to the way you seek to justify yourself with God. One day a young prophet came to these men and told them that they did not need to dwell in this old barn, in the semidarkness. He said they could come out in the sunlight. But these men refused to believe him, and in anger put him to death. Later on some of them did take the young prophet's word, and went outside to live. But the light was too strong, and so they erected against that light a series of umbrellas. Those umbrellas are simply the excuses we erect against Jesus. But he comes clothed in love to judge.

And if you—like the Jewish leaders—want evidence of his authority, our Lord gave a cryptic clue. It is the last truth our sign points to.

Something About Our Future

In answer to the Jewish leaders' question for a sign of his authority, Jesus replied, "Destroy this temple, and in three days I will raise it up" (2:19). The Jews were incredulous. Literal-minded, they thought only of the splendid Temple Herod had taken forty-six years to build.

But now John's reportorial intent comes into full view. He was giving us a benefit the Jews did not have. Wrote John: "But he spoke of the temple of his body. When therefore he was raised from the dead, his disciples remembered that he said this; and they believed the scripture and the word which Jesus had spoken" (2:21–22, RSV)

We live on the after side of Jesus' resurrection, as John also came to do. Because of the resurrection, we can see Jesus' truth validated. His actions, as reported in John 2, point to the truth of both joy and judgment in religion. The wedding wine is a sign of the true joy in Jesus; the Temple cleansing speaks of Jesus' judgment on bad religion.

The Temple cleansing as a sign also is convincingly personal. It tells us something about ourselves we need to know: the tendency in matters of religious faith to let the bad drive out the good. It tells us something about our Savior: He comes in love and judgment to deliver us from that which our worst side would deliver us to. And it tells us something about our future: There is a resurrection in it for those who know true joy in Jesus.

6 Out of the Night

John 3:1–10; 7:45–52; 19:38–42

We cannot help but wonder who reported this conversation. Only two principals were involved. One was Jesus; the other, Nicodemus. We can be sure that John the gospelist did not get his material from Jesus. The conversation was confidential, and Jesus would never betray a confidence. Perhaps the clue to its source is found in John 7:45–52 and 19:38–42. In those passages we discover Nicodemus' further involvement in Jesus' cause, climaxing in his claiming Jesus' body after the crucifixion. With this weaving of Nicodemus' story into the unfolding Gospel account, could we not conclude that the source for this conversation may have been Nicodemus himself?

The conversation moves through three levels. These levels could be described as questions. The first of the questions is only implied. Nicodemus asks Jesus inferentially, "Where have you come from?" The query is behind the opening statement, "Rabbi, we know that you are a teacher come from God; for no one can do these signs that you do, unless God is with him" (v. 2). So, the first question is, "Did you come from God?"

The second question is, "How can a man be born when he is old? How can one have the kind of experience you speak of?"

The third question is, "How can this happen [to me]?"

These questions are in order. The first is the *rhetorical*

question, which is asked as a matter of courtesy: "Where did you come from, Jesus?" The second is the *objective* question, in which Nicodemus asked for information: "How can a man be born from above?" The third question is intimate, personal, *subjective:* "How can this happen to me?" Here we have a conversation which begins man to man, continues mind to mind, and concludes heart to heart.

A study in contrast can be found in the meeting of Jesus and Nicodemus. On the one hand is the young, peripatetic prophet from the despised province of Galilee, and that more despised town called Nazareth. Jesus is an outsider, outlander, imposing by his teachings and works his presence upon the center of Jewish religious life. One of the religious leaders has come to engage him in conversation. In all likelihood, Nicodemus did not come on his own. He may have been a kind of committee of one. His opening remark was, "*We* know. . . ." Evidently, Jesus had been the subject of conversation in a meeting of the Sanhedrin. Perhaps, out of curiosity Nicodemus had volunteered to engage Jesus in this interogatory conversation.

So, we have the young man confronted by the old man. The young man, without any credentials but himself; the old man, heavy with stature, reputation, and substance. They have come face to face; man to man.

The New Birth Is a Must

"Rabbi—teacher—we know you are a teacher come from God. We'll admit that. We've seen what you've done. No man can do what you've done unless God is with him." An ordinary man would have been knocked off balance by such a tribute. A finer compliment could not have been passed by a part of the religious establishment on an outsider. But in response, Jesus very abruptly says, "You, Nicodemus, must be born from above." Or translated another way, "You, Nicodemus, must be born again." (The Greek word *anothen* can be translated either way; the translation depends on the context.) Jesus was affirming the fact that this birth from above is a must; an absolute necessity.

The new birth is a necessity because of the way we are. It is a necessity because of the conflict we experience in our inner lives. No man on the face of the earth was more religious than Saul of Tarsus. Yet, on one occasion, as he looked at his own inner life, he wrote: "I observe then a principle in me that when I would do good, evil is near at hand. . . . The good that I would, I do not; the evil that I would not, I do." (See Rom. 7:21,19.) Which one of us could honestly say, "This is not true of me"? It is an unvarying principle: The virtue we would like to achieve we can never quite bring off, try as we will. Apart from grace, an estrangement from God seems to deepen as life prolongs. So Thomas Hood rightly wrote:

I remember, I remember
The house where I was born,
The little windows where the sun
Came peeping in at morn;
It never came a wink too soon
Nor brought too long a day;
But now, I often wish the night
Had borne my breath away.

I remember, I remember
The fir-trees dark and high;
I used to think their slender tops
Were close against the sky:
It was a childish ignorance,
But now 'tis little joy
To know I'm farther off from Heaven
Than when I was a boy.

Hood describes the human experience apart from God and the grace he has extended in Jesus Christ. To this prominent, substantial member of the religious establishment called Nicodemus, Jesus therefore said, "Nicodemus, you must be born again."

The New Birth Is a Miracle

One of the characteristics of John's Gospel is his use of symbolism. When John wrote, "This man came to Jesus by night" he likely meant the statement to be understood, "This man came to Jesus *out of* night." John described a spiritual state as well as a temporal fact.

Evidence of that intention is found in the next movement of the conversation. Earlier we noted the ambiguity of the word *anothen;* it can mean "from above" or "again," depending upon the context. Had Nicodemus been of the light, and not the night, he might have responded to *anothen* on the spiritual plane. But he did not. Instead, Nicodemus took *anothen* to refer to a physical experience. Hence, his question, "How can a man be born when he is old? Can he enter a second time into his mother's womb and be born?"

Thinking as he did, Nicodemus asks the obvious question. It is the objective question; he seeks facts, he seeks information: "How can a man like myself, old, be born *anothen?* Is it possible for me to enter my mother's womb a second time and be born?" And Jesus replied to what may have been a condescending, even sarcastic question: "Nicodemus, unless you are born of the water and the Spirit you cannot enter the kingdom of God."

This is the miracle of the new birth. This new life that God gives is God's gift. We cannot rightly relate ourselves to God by our own efforts, our energy, our reformation, or our good works. We relate ourselves rightly to God through receiving that gift God gives by his Spirit. God's first gift to us is physical life. God wants also to give us spiritual life. Entry into God's kingdom comes as his gracious gift. We receive that gift through faith and in repentance.

So David, after he had sinned with Bathsheba, rightly prayed, "Create in me a clean heart, O God, and put a new and right spirit within me" (Ps. 51:10, RSV).

The New Birth Is a Spiritual Reality

The conversation moved on then from the informational to the personal level. Jesus went on to say, "Nicodemus, you and I know that, on the physical level, the wind blows as it wills. We cannot tell whence it came or whither it goes. This also is the way with the new birth."

Now, in Jesus' day there were no TV weather forecasters who drew maps and traced the movements of weather fronts, the highs and the lows, and the various meteorological factors affecting weather. In that more primitive day, all weather came from God, as they understood it. And the wind was the breath of God. They had but one word for "wind" and "breath" and "spirit." In Jesus' explanation of the new birth, he used the same word (*pneuma*) with reference to wind and Spirit. So when Jesus spoke to Nicodemus, he used the one word *pneuma* interchangeably for wind and Spirit. By his usage, Jesus emphasized the fact that the spiritual reality—the new birth—is God's work.

"How am I born again?" That was Nicodemus' question. The answer was: "Nicodemus, you accept this gift from God even as you accept the wind and the weather. When you open your life to this gift from God, his Spirit moves in. When his Spirit moves in, the effect of that experience is expressed in your life—in your actions, in your commitment, in your values."

Did Nicodemus submit to the Spirit? We noted earlier that John in his Gospel made two other references to Nicodemus. One is found in John 7:45–52. In a meeting of the Sanhedrin the officers came back to explain their failure to arrest Jesus. Very gingerly, tentatively, Nicodemus came to Jesus and the soldiers' defense.

The second reference is in John 19:38–42. Much had happened. Jesus had been arrested, tried, condemned, and crucified. His body hung on the cross, with no one to claim it. Two old men in the city—Joseph of Arimathea and Nicodemus—met. Joseph said to Nicodemus, "Look, Nick. Do you feel as I do about Jesus?"

"I don't know how you feel, Joe, but if you feel as I think you do, then, yes, I feel as you do."

"Well, then, let's go to Pilate, and let's ask permission to take Jesus' body down before sundown and give him a decent burial."

Can you imagine? Here was a man who came out of night to talk to Jesus at first. He had, a little later, timidly defended Jesus in the Sanhedrin. But now, after the authorities had done their worst, he went publicly to claim that cross and him who hung on it as his very own. No more open identification with Jesus could have been made.

Nicodemus had asked the question, "How can this happen to me?" In his action is evidence he had understood and acted. He opened his heart; the Spirit had moved; and John recorded the effect. Christina Rossetti has a poem, "The Wind," that expresses the spiritual reality of the new birth of the Spirit, made known by the effects produced:

> Who has seen the wind?
> Neither I nor you.
> But when the leaves hang trembling,

The wind is passing through.
Who has seen the wind?
Neither you nor I.
But when the trees bow down their heads,
The wind is passing by.

Nicodemus came in out of night into God's kingdom of glorious light. Have you?

7 A Changed World
John 4:4–30

The woman in our Scripture passage could step out of the New Testament into our twentieth-century world and be right at home, so far as mood and morality go. She had a civil war going on inside her, and so do many of us.

At least, that is what the late Dr. Karl Menninger of the famed Menninger Clinic has told us. He wrote that mental or emotional illness affects "one out of one of us"; that we simply do not recognize it. We do have names for the more severe cases: "nervous breakdown," "combat fatigue," or "shell shock." But, he goes on, what we do not recognize is that many of the common complaints are also evidence of mental and emotional stress. And he cites "tension headache," "marital discords," "nicotine or alcohol addiction," "business worries" as some of the evidences of inner turmoil and conflict that rage on the inside all the time.

Well, if that is the hallmark of our time, then this woman—worldly-wise, experienced, articulate, aggressive—really belonged. She had lost most of her virtues, including the virtue of reverence. She had drifted into a self-defeating cycle of defiance, self-recrimination, and even bolder defiance. She was caught in the paralysis of what Victor Frankl would call an "existential vacuum"—a descending spiral of conflict and meaninglessness. So let's look at this story in which we find the modern so faithfully mirrored.

It is pretty remarkable, when you come to think of it, that the form given this conversation is something like a transcription. Especially is that true when John took no pains to hide the fact that none of them were there until it was all over (4:8,27). And if we add to that the fact that this was put in written form some fifty years later, it dawns on us that we have here a kind of reconstruction of a conversation. It is not a verbatim report; it is a resumé; an approximation.

There is no question, however, that the conversation took place. It is too geniune, too much in keeping with the character of our Savior to doubt it. And the woman is geniune, too. Nothing about her has a counterfeit ring.

As we follow the conversation, it seems to divide itself into at least three major movements. At the first (a very brief section) we find reflected the *external conflicts* of the day. Here are the artificial conventions men have erected by which they wall one another out. But Jesus deftly penetrates those obstacles and moves to the *inner conflicts* in the woman's life. (This is a longer passage.) For those who have some artistic imagination, it would not be hard to visualize a kind of choreography for this second part. Jesus made a feint; she adroitly evaded. But with each manuever she gave ground and at last she fell before her pursuer. The final passage is the resolution of conflict.

But this conversation is more than choreography; it is the prelude to an armistice in a civil war. Here is the struggle of a soul finding itself, confronted as she was by the eternal in Jesus. And through it all is the witness of John that Jesus is the master peacemaker, putting back together the broken fragments of a shattered person living in a broken world. He is in the business of making people whole again.

External Conflicts

The opening of the story is ordinary enough, except for one clue which John gave at the very beginning. The clue consists of just six words, one brief sentence, but it set up the intended mood of suspense. Here it is: "He must needs go through Samaria" (4:4). That is the clue; it helps us understand what is to follow.

Now Samaria was a Jewish no-man's land. To travel through Samaria was unthinkable by any self-respecting Jew. You can imagine, then, the horror attached to the idea of accepting Samaritan hospitality.

The Jews felt they had their reasons. For one thing, the Samaritans had betrayed the racial purity of Jewish lineage. Long before Jesus' time they had dismissed the idea of keeping Jewish blood unmixed. They had engaged in racial intermarriage for hundreds of years. The Jews thought of the Samaritans as mongrels.

And even more offensive was their corruption of Jewish faith. For nearly a millennium the Samaritans had been engaged in religious syncretism. They took elements of the pagan religions and incorporated them into their own worship.

For these reasons and more the Jews despised the Samaritans. Here was an age-old conflict, and every generation had added a little more to the accumulation of enmity, recrimination, and bitterness. Even those who had forgotten why had not forgotten that "the Jews have no dealings with the Samaritans." It was a byword. But Jesus had dealings with the Samaritans. And in the midst of his dealings with this one Samaritan we have this conversation.

It is midday when the conversation opened. Our Lord and his disciples had been traveling all morning long. They were hot, dusty, and thirsty. They would have gotten a drink, all of them, there at the well of Jacob on the outskirts of Sychar if they only had a container of some kind. But they did not. So while the disciples went into town to get some food and water Jesus stayed by the well to rest.

As Jesus waited, a woman from the village approached the well. He noticed her, and probably thought, "This is strange; coming here at midday. What is she running from?" She was aggressive, bold. She was undaunted by the presence of this strange man. She knew men; knew how to handle them. He was no threat to her. An opportunity, perhaps, but no threat.

And Jesus broke the barrier of silence. "Give me a drink," he said. She bristled. She was haughty, knowledgeable. "Humph! How come you, a Jew, ask me, a Samaritan, for a drink? You know the conventions." (That is not exactly how John reported it; it does catch the spirit.)

But already Jesus had penetrated the artificial barriers that would have kept them at arms' length. He, a man, had spoken to her, a woman. Moreover, he had suggested that he be allowed to drink out of her water skin—an unthinkable breach of convention. And even more bold: he was a Jew; she a Samaritan!

There is nothing new about such conventions. They are an all-too-human tendency; the tendency to wall out what we do not understand, what we do not know. There are invisible walls in your world and mine, too. We Protestants have a tendency to wall out Catholics; we whites have a yen to wall out the blacks; the white collars the blue collars; the liberals the conservatives. Sometimes a husband walls out his wife, and vice versa. But Jesus came into our world to bring down walls (Eph. 2:14), and that is exactly what he was doing here.

Here he was a Jew talking to a Samaritan; a man talking to a woman because he wanted to bring these unnatural walls down. They were both needing the same thing—water. The woman apparently got the point of it, and she stuck around to see what such a remarkable person would have to say to her.

The Inner Conflict

The next part of the conversation is rather long. Jesus never answered her question in so many words. Instead, he let his geniune interest in her as a person, his refusal to treat her as a nonperson, be answer enough. He moved in swiftly and boldly.

I must remark in passing on the initiative of Jesus in this conversation. Unlike some of our modern counselors and psychiatrists, Jesus has a definite and immediate goal in mind. He did not want to make this woman comfortable; he wanted to make her well. He accepted the idea that pain goes along with healing, and that they had better get the healing process started. So often the modern psychiatrist dispenses tranquilizers and the counsel to withdraw from the world. That may be all right if one wants to cling precariously on the brink of life, a nonfunctioning shadow of a real person. But Jesus aims to put us squarely in the mainstream of life.

So he took one bold leap and landed squarely in the middle of her inner turmoil. He did it by talking to the woman about water, having already asked her for a drink. At the first, the woman was terribly confused, and quite rightly. She took him literally. She was what the psychologist would call "reality-bound."

But not for long. She soon caught on that there were higher overtones to this conversation; that Jesus had moved beyond the merely physical level to that inner world where all her furniture was in motley disarray. And then she heard Jesus say, "If you would ask me, I could give you a drink that would really satisfy" (see v. 10).

Although she sensed the overtones, she wanted to avoid them. She talked about how deep the well was; how he had nothing to draw with; how the well had provided water from Jacob's time on down. (See vv. 11–12.)

Patiently, Jesus made his offer again. This time, her defenses relaxed but not down, she said (somewhat tentatively), "Well, give me some of that water."

And now Jesus began to open up to her just what this armistice would require: "Go, call your husband." Is that not Jesus' way of saying that when we hear the gospel call we must begin where we are? that it is useless to breast-beat over an irrecoverable past? that it is better to look forward than to look backward? to make a new pattern rather than repeat the old all over again?

But such a suggestion involved some radical changes for the woman. She had to give up being so self-centered, so demanding. Possibly she was going to have to put her relationship to the man in her life on an altogether different basis. She sensed this, and immediately the defenses went back up.

She was clever. The question she asked was a religious question. That is one of the most natural things in the world—to raise some theoretical question when we are face to face with a deep inner demand that God has put upon us. It is a favorite diversionary tactic. So we criticize the church, the music, the preacher, the officers, the program. That is so much easier than to straighten out the mess that cries for mending.

But Jesus would not be distracted. He dismissed the

whole shopworn business, telling her that *where* we worship is not important; it is *who* we worship, and how. Self on the throne always leads to idolatrous worship. And idolatrous worship confirms us in our worst features.

And now she knew that this was authentic. This was her moment of truth. But it was an anguish-filled moment, and she would avoid it if she could. She had one more tactic: "I know that one day the Messiah will come and he will straighten out everything."

How like us—to push out into the future this pressing matter that needs decision now! To say with Agrippa "some more convenient season" is the most humanly natural thing to do in all the world. It is also the most damning.

So Jesus brought her face to face with a reality that rocked her world, and will rock yours and mine when we really take it in fully. Said Jesus, "I that speaketh to thee am he."

Do you know how they catch live monkeys in the jungle? Jars are hung in the trees, each jar having a long, narrow neck, and inside the jar a small red rubber ball. A monkey finds a jar, and out of curiosity he reaches his hand into the jar and grasps the ball. But when he tries to pull his fist out, it won't come. The monkey desperately wants to get loose but is not willing to let go of the red ball; so he becomes a captive for life.

Do you know anybody like that? A person who wants deliverance from all his problems and from the emptiness of his life, but who is not willing to turn loose of the things that are holding him back? Is it you who remains a captive, yet despising yourself for it?

Apparently, the Samaritan woman faced up to herself.

The Conflict Resolved

In the rest of the story, it is not what the woman said that is important; it is what she did. We are told just how different this woman's world became. The very people she had avoided she now brought to Jesus. The edginess, the hostility, the defensiveness in her life seemed to have evaporated. Her world, which had been so fractured and broken, came together with a wholeness she had never dreamed possible.

Is not this the story of any person who brings his guilt and his brokenness to the Savior?

We have been looking at a conversation about inner conflict. All the while we have considered the Samaritan woman's conflict with the top of our minds, but it is our own conflict that really concerns us. I come to you, as an ambassador of the Great Physician, to say that he can change your world, too. All you need do is set forth in the words of a simple and beloved old hymn, "I Lay My Sins on Jesus," by Horatius Bonar.

> I lay my sins on Jesus, the spotless Lamb of God;
> He bears them all, and frees us from the accursed load;
> I bring my guilt to Jesus, to wash my crimson stains
> White in His blood most precious, till not a stain remains.
>
> I lay my wants on Jesus; all fulness dwells in him;
> He heals all my diseases, he doth my soul redeem:
> I lay my griefs on Jesus, my burdens and my cares;
> He from them all releases, he all my sorrows shares.

8 At the Circle's Edge
John 4:46–54

Few of us, perhaps none of us, has had the experience Katherine Mansfield wrote about in her journal. She was in the midst of a valiant but futile struggle with disease. After her death at the age of thirty-four her friends found in her journal these thoughts:

> I should like this to be accepted as my confession. There is no limit to human suffering. When one thinks, "Now I have touched the bottom of the sea—now I can go no deeper," one does go deeper. But I do not want to die without leaving a record of my belief that suffering can be overcome. For I do believe it.

That is the kind of experience I mean by the words "circle's edge." These are the boundary experiences, and they test people's mettle.

Perhaps that last thought is the reason John included this second Cana story in his Gospel. It is about a man whom John identified as an "official," but whom Matthew (8:5–13) and Luke (7:1–10) called "centurion." The evangel John used this miracle as a "second sign that Jesus did when he had come from Judea to Galilee" (v. 54).

Three phrases seem to catch and tell the story: first, an unusual need; second, an unusual faith; and third, an unusual result.

An Unusual Need

The extent of the need in the story is caught in the

phrase "for he was at the point of death" (v. 47, RSV), a phrase used to describe the centurion's sick servant. Psychologists call this one of life's boundary experiences. Such times make a profound impression on us, as Edgar A. Guest has portrayed in a stanza of his poem on making a house a home:

> Ye've got to weep t' make it home;
> ye've got to sit an sigh
> An' watch beside a loved one's bed
> An' know that death is nigh.
> An' in the stillness of the night
> T' see Death's angel come
> An' still the hands o' her ye loved,
> An' make her sweet voice dumb.
> Tis scenes like these that touch the heart
> An' when yer tears are dried,
> Home's dearer than it was before, an' sorta sanctified.

The centurion's servant was sick unto death.

We do not know for sure the exact date of John's writing, but most students fix it in the decade A.D. 90–100. If that is correct, then the church may have felt an unusual need. Peter and Paul were dead; struck down by the unreasoning villany of mad Nero. After a time of smoldering fires, persecution had broken into an open conflagration under the despotic Domitian, who murdered unnumbered innocent Christians. Some attribute his senseless rage to the infiltration of his own household by the Christian faith. The year A.D. 93 is marked in infamy as Domitian's bloodbath at Christians' expense.

Whatever the immediate scene, this story must have spoken to human need then, as it does now. For need, unusual need, is always some Christian's lot.

An Unusual Faith

Many forces conspired to discourage this centurion's belief that Jesus could help. Racial difference, physical distance, religious dogma—all these were present, and any one of them would have stopped most of us. Matthew recorded Jesus as saying of the centurion, "Truly, I say to you, not even in Israel have I found such faith" (8:10). The centurion, as a man in authority himself, dared to believe that Jesus' authority could conquer distance, dogma, and racial difference.

One of John's key words in his Gospel is the word *believe.* He used some form of the word ninety-eight times—40 percent of the New Testament usage of that word. Moreover, when John used the word he was describing an active commitment. In this story, "the man believed the word that Jesus spoke" (v. 50).

We have been raised on the scientific method: formulate the hypothesis; conduct the experiments; tabulate the results; draw a conclusion. That approach has sifted down into the wisdom of the proverb, and we say, "Seeing is believing." Some, like Andrew, Nathaniel, and Thomas can do no better than that. They have to investigate before they can believe. They have to accumulate the evidence. Well, God accepts us as we are and where we are, and he will take us on those terms if he must. He took Andrew, John, Nathaniel, and Thomas that way.

But when it comes to trusting God, there is a sense in which we must believe to see. Abraham did. To Thomas, who did not, and to second- and third-generation Christians for whom the going was rough—as well as for ourselves—the evangel John recorded Jesus as saying, "Blessed are those who have not seen and yet believe" (20:29, RSV).

The Roman centurion was one of those, and he is a sign because of his unusual faith.

An Unusual Result

John reported the result of the centurion's faith with a sparse economy: "Yesterday at the seventh hour the fever left him" (v. 52). One minute the servant was at death's door; the next, he was recovering. And when the centurion compared notes with the folks at home, he discovered that the recovery occurred when Jesus spoke the creative word.

Sometimes faith gets a different answer from that which the centurion received. Sometimes, like Paul's answer, it comes to us this way: "My grace is sufficient for you, for my power is made perfect in weakness."

But whether it be recovery, or God's power made perfect in our weakness, the truth of this sign is the same: power to cope or power to overcome is from God. When you are on the circle's edge, and you look into the abyss, this Gospel story comes as "sign" of a heartening truth:

Peace does not mean the end of all our striving,
  Joy does not mean the drying of our tears;
Peace is the power that comes to souls arriving
  Up to the light where God Himself appears.

Joy is the wine that God is ever pouring
  Into the hearts of those who strive with Him,
Light'ning their eyes to vision and adoring,
  Strength'ning their arms to warfare glad and grim.

G. A. STUDDERT-KENNEDY

9 Stand Up and Be Counted

John 5:2–10

It was a feast day. Which one, we are not sure. John never bothered to name it. Just put it down that the occasion was special.

The controversy between Jesus and the Pharisees had been growing. It centered on sabbath observance. John waited until this point to tell that part of the story, but then we have already seen that John used his materials selectively. The other Gospel writers had already "set down in order" the events of Jesus' ministry. The other Evangelists tell us how Jesus defended his casual attitude toward the sabbath—casual so far as the Pharisees were concerned. Jesus put human need ahead of the sabbath (Luke 13:10–17); he had cited King David's precedent (Mark 2:23–28); he had reminded the Pharisees of the priestly exemption (Matt. 12:5). When we get to this point in Jesus' life as covered by John's story, the controversy has assumed full-blown proportions.

On this particular feast day Jesus did not go up to the Temple, not this day. He went to one of the local healing shrines, called Bethesda, which means "house of healing." This shrine had its own reputation which amounted to not much more than ignorant superstition. The local folks believed that the mysteriously churning pool could be explained by the visitation of an angel. Five porches had been built all around this thermal pool, and the floors of those porches were strewn with the lame, blind, and paralyzed. It was sight enough to wring the heart of an ogre—all that suffering and misery gathered in one place.

When Jesus stepped up on those porches, no one noticed. Every eye was on the pool. It was about time for the water to stir, and each watched with hope. Jesus swept his eyes across that mass of human misery, and approaching the man of our story, asked, "Do you want to get well?"

What a question! Why else was he there? "Do you want to get well?" Of course he did! And then came the explanation: he had been sick thirty-eight years (a symbol of the duration of the wilderness wanderings?); he was paralyzed; no one would help him into the water; somebody else always beat him to the miracle; but he kept coming back. That was his answer. In effect, he was saying, "Yes, sir. I want to be well. What I need is someone to help me."

What he did not know was that he had found that one.

Three perspectives for our own horizons I would draw from this sign. The first is the fact of the helpless person. The second is the hindrance, symbolized by the sabbath. The third is the responsible human being the invalid became. In these three perspectives our story is comprised, our truth comprehended.

The Helpless Person

Jesus' question to the paralyzed man was direct: "Do you want to be healed?" That question goes to the heart of the matter: How *willing* are you to be helped? The first step the Savior takes is to get from us our free and open consent to be helped. And this consent people do not always give.

Could I name some reasons why?

Sometimes people hang back because *they do not know any better*. That was the case of the invalid of the story.

When we find him he is in the thralldom of a local superstition. He is waiting for the brush of an angel's wing, and he has been waiting for thirty-eight years. He was doing what he had learned.

Wilma Dykman in her book *Prophet of Plenty* tells of a young Virginia woman who had come to spend a summer at W. D. Weatherford's Blue Ridge Lodge on the outskirts of Asheville, North Carolina. It was the rule of the lodge that everyone had to study; everyone had to work. This young woman had been assigned the task of waiting on tables. At the first meal, however, her table was unattended. Weatherford searched her out; found her in her room, crying. "I just can't do that," she sobbed. "Can't do what?" asked Weatherford. "I can't serve table. That is what niggers do in my home." [1]

We may not know any better, but if we are willing Jesus can help us.

Sometimes people hang back because *they are no better*. Strange creatures we are, capable of angelic loveliness and devilish caprice. A bit of doggerel speaks to this contradiction in us with disarmingly simple lines:

> I'm a man, and man's a mixture,
> Right from his very birth;
> Part of him comes from heaven,
> But part of him comes from earth.[2]

We are a house divided. Paul speaks of the carnal and the spiritual, but the division is more complex than that. We are *prisoners of history*—our own and our world's—yet we live in the present and the future. We walk on the ground but gaze at the stars.

We are *individuals*, yet we are part of the human race, living in a complex webb of interrelatedness that confronts us with both awe and horror.

We are *free,* yet we are set in a context of "givenness" over which we had no voice and no veto.

We can *create,* but we also destroy. So the husband who helps create life also helps destroy and scar the life of his own child by his lack of self-discipline and self-control. Oscar Wilde observed that about us in the "Ballad of Reading Gaol":

> Yet each man kills the things he loves
> By each let this be heard,
> Some do it with a bitter look,
> Some with a flattering word,
> The coward does it with a kiss,
> The brave man with a sword!

The apostle Paul marked this strange ambivalence, and defined it for all of us: "I find then a law, that, when I would do good, evil is present with me. . . . wretched man that I am! Who shall deliver me from this body of death?" (Rom. 7:21–24).

And sometimes people are not helped because *they want no better.* Some of us *will* to be less and to accomplish less than God meant for us to. We count avoidance of stress as a good, and choose the evil of dying with most of our music still in us.

When Jesus had healed the paralyzed man, he sought him out and said, "See, you are well! Sin no more, that nothing worse befall you" (see John 5:14, RSV).

What did Jesus mean by that? Whatever else, I think he meant for him to be a person, with all that implies. He wanted him to affirm his powers; to accept responsibility for himself and his world; to fulfill the ancient command: Have dominion! Jesus was warning him that to weasel out—to be less than a responsible person—was to commit the sin of sloth; to "renounce the claim implicit in his human dignity."

The Hindrance

The second perspective of this sign is the hindrance, symbolized by the sabbath. In consequence of the paralyzed man's boon a further conflict between Jesus and the Pharisees developed. The Pharisees sensed a threat in Jesus, a threat to their way of life.

Jesus lay bare the heart of the conflict when he asked, "How can you believe, who receive glory from one another and do not seek the glory that comes from the only God?" (5:44, RSV).

They were busy passing glory back and forth to one another; so busy they could not see the wonder and glory of Jesus. He was nothing more than an intruder; a threat to them; somebody who would come in and break up their playhouse. That was the hindrance—their self-interest which blocked God's power.

They kept their sabbath and rejected the Savior. I cannot help but recount that within forty years they lost the very thing they were trying to save. The Temple went down into dust. Wasn't it Jesus who said, in effect: "If you try to save yourself, you'll lose out; but if you will lose yourself for my sake and the gospel's, you'll save everything"? (See Mark 8:35.) The Pharisees are a case in point.

A Full Human Being

We have spoken of the helpless person; of the hindrance. There is another perspective in the story, the invalid. Saturated as he was in his ignorance, helplessness, and superstition, he stated his plight in the pathetic words, "Sir, I have no man to help me."

Jesus changed all that, of course, both for the man and

for us. He wants us to let him help us realize our full personhood as functioning, sensitive, responsible human beings.

Are you willing for him to do that with you?

Some years ago I received a letter from a student nurse who was in our young people's Training Union at the time. She was irregular in her attendance because of her nursing duties, but she had come one Sunday evening, and the letter followed. I quote part of it.

> In the work we are doing we must know God well. For instance—we had a man here in contagion a month ago. He didn't know God. When we realized that his time was near (Blastomycosis—a rare, fatal, fungus disease), the supervisor called a minister who left him a Testament. No one offered to read it to him the next day—so that night I read him some passages from Romans, John, Corinthians. I talked to him about his need for God. I did this every night for a week. The night he died I read him a passage out of John—thirty-nine minutes before death took him. When I came on duty the next day Miss Ida, an aide, asked who had been talking to him. Before he died he had told Miss Ida to call for his brother. He said, "Tell him I'm ready to go." You just can't imagine how good I felt inside knowing I had helped someone find God.

I think the paralyzed man would understand that letter. It was written by a young woman who, like him, had learned to become a responsible human being in a world of need.

10 Hidden Hunger

John 6:4–14

This story is one of the best reported incidents in the life of Jesus. It must have made a tremendous impression on our Lord's followers. Matthew (14:13–21), Mark (6:30–44), and Luke (9:10–17) reported it similarly. But John gave it his own unique interpretation, for to John it was a "sign."

For one thing, John brings out an aspect of the setting which the other evangels omitted. For them the important fact was that John the Baptist had been killed by Herod Antipas, and the people had thronged around Jesus because they were upset. John disregarded that fact; for him the important prop in the backdrop was the Passover (6:4): "And the passover, a feast of the Jews, was nigh." John included the insights of the other gospel writers, but then went on to use this quiet little detail of the story to make a unique point. We shall see that meaning of this "sign" a bit later.

The first-century church recognized the insight of John; his special contribution to the proper understanding of Jesus. They took his writing as God's Word, too, and it has come to stand in our New Testaments right alongside the straightforward reporting of the other gospelists. It comes to us today as God's Word for our here and now.

As such, I would share with you three truths from John's version of the miraculous breaking of bread on Galilee's shores. First is the suggestion of the wrong use of Jesus.

Second is the subtle thought of how much Jesus can do with our little. The first two truths can be found in all the versions of the incident, but this last is especially John's insight: Only Jesus can provide food for our hidden hunger.

Wrong Uses of Jesus

As has been noted, John quietly inserted at the very beginning of his account the fact that the Passover season was at hand. Now the Passover was the Jews' Fourth of July and Easter all rolled into one. It celebrated their national beginnings as well as their revival of hope. Passover marked the beginning of the exodus from Egypt. They had been marking this national event for more than fourteen hundred years. But it had become a distasteful observance, even humiliating. The past eighty-nine annual holidays had been marked under the watchful eye of the Roman soldier. What Judea needed was a new birth of freedom. They were on the lookout for a new "George Washington," or in their own jargon, a new Moses.

You can understand their excitement, then, when they discovered that the bread Jesus gave them was his own manna from heaven. Here was a new Moses (v. 14, see Deut. 18:15,18), replete with a self-contained bakery! A mere spark would ignite their enthusiasm into a real fire of pent-up patriotism. "Roman, go home!" could become more than a slogan; it might become an order.

To prevent such precipitous action Jesus slipped off by himself into the hills. The next day, with the crowd still pursuing, Jesus pricked the balloon of their expectation with a quick thrust: "You are looking for me now not because you saw my signs but because you ate that food and had all you wanted" (v. 25, Phillips). In effect, Jesus said, "You're not interested in me for what I am; for what I stand for. You are following me because of what you think you may be able to get out of me."

Jesus had them pegged, all right. He saw right through them. They were hoping to use Jesus. That offends us, perhaps, because it finds us. We sometimes want to turn Jesus to our own good, too, if we can just find the way.

A Lot with a Little

A second truth drawn from this sign is a lesson the apostles, especially Philip learned about their Master on this day.

Our Lord's eye may have twinkled when he asked Philip: "How are we going to feed all these people?" If so, Philip never caught it; he took himself and the situation too seriously. Rather, Philip ran over to Judas, took a quick check on the status of their treasury, and came back wagging his head. We are not told the treasurer's report, but calculating on the basis of a day's wage at forty dollars, Philip had figured out that it would take two hundred workdays' wages, or about eight thousand dollars, to feed the crowd. That was assuming they could find a bakery with the facilities to bake the bread necessary.

Some of us are like Philip—always depreciating what we have, and appreciating what we need. But not everyone reacts that way, thank goodness. While Philip was dolefully recounting their meager resources, Andrew had gone out in the crowd and found a boy with a lunch. You know that lovely story; you've heard many a sermon on it, and you may have taught a lesson or two from it. But perhaps we need to read the lesson of the sign once again: Jesus can take what little we have, and he can do with it more than we can imagine.

When General Booth, the founder of the Salvation

Army, was asked for the secret of his success in London's East End (that place where the social experimenters had dismally failed), he replied that God had had all there was of him. He went on to speak of how other men may have had greater opportunities, but from the day he had gotten the poor of London's East End on his heart, and a vision of what Christ could do for them, he had made up his mind that God could have all there was of him.

God can do a lot with a little.

Food for Hidden Hunger

Now let's turn in an altogether different direction. This sign of John's, in the context of the Passover and the people's expectation of a new Moses, becomes under John's artistry a means for pointing to the primacy of the spiritual in our lives.

John reported Jesus as saying midway in the discourse on the sign's meaning: "Your fathers ate the manna in the wilderness, and they died. . . . I am the living bread" (6:49–51, RSV).

Jesus was saying to these secularists of his day: "Our forebears wanted the very kind of thing you want. They got it, but they are all dead. You will be too, and the bread you ate will pass back to the ground from whence it came. Your real need is bread for your hidden hunger; food for your inner man."

It touches me with sadness to see how prone we are to center life in that which passes, while that which counts eternally is often neglected. Are you like this one?

> There was a man in our town
> And he had wondrous health,
> But recklessly he squandered it
> Accumulating wealth.

So when, at last, his health was gone,
  With all his might and main,
He turned around and spent his wealth
  To get his health again.

And then, when, with neither health nor wealth
  He in his coffin lay—
The preacher couldn't say a word,
  Excepting, "Let us pray." [1]

But how salvage something of value from the passing scene? I think Jesus gave the clue we look for in the discourse on this sign. He said, "I am the living bread." It was his way of saying that we must make him the center of life; let everything we do find its place and meaning in relation to him; let him give life meaning. Take Christ in your life, and the hidden hunger will be satisifed.

11 Safe at Sea
John 6:16–21

Joseph Conrad spins a tale called "Typhoon," a story about Captain MacWhirr, his ship the *Nan-Shan*, and a storm on the China Sea. The captain, Conrad relates, had been sailing the high seas all his life. But he never did comprehend the enormity of the approaching storm, although during the crucial hours before the typhoon hit, he had warnings. While he should have been tying down his cargo, and readying the crew, the captain stared solidly at the falling barometer in sheer unbelief, refusing to comprehend and act on what his mind received as warning. He had never known the sea in its capacity for fury. He could not believe it was happening now. Conrad wrote of the Captain's reactions to the storm warnings thus:

> The sea itself had never put itself out to startle the silent man, who seldom looked up and wandered innocently over the waters with the only visible purpose of getting food, raiment, and houseroom for three people ashore. Dirty weather he had known, of course. He had been made wet, uncomfortable, tired in the usual way, felt at the time and presently forgotten. So that upon the whole he had been justified in reporting fine weather at home. But he had never been given a glimpse of immeasurable strength and of immoderate wrath, the wrath that passes exhausted but never appeased—the wrath and fury of the passionate sea. He knew it existed, as we know that crime and abominations exist; he had heard of it as a peaceable citizen in a town hears of battles, famines, and floods, and yet knows nothing of what these things mean—though, indeed, he may have been mixed up in a street row, have gone without his dinner once, or been soaked to the skin in a shower.[1]

So when the storm struck, the two hundred Chinese coolies in the ship's hold were pounded into a mass of misery by the inferno of careening, catapulting cargo and gear that had never been secured. The captain, the ship, the crew, the cargo—all were at the mercy of the sea.

Sometimes life seems to be like that. We go along on reasonably moderate seas for a long time, observing the grief that comes to others, yet somehow always managing to bring off our own skirmishes with danger and disaster. But then it seems that life itself conspires against us. With an immoderate passion, a vague and impersonal fury seems to descend upon us. Wave upon wave roll over us, exhausting us, but themselves unappeased. And we—like Captain MacWhirr—are at the mercy of the elements.

When this little story which I have called "Safe at Sea" was first made a part of the written Gospel, the Christians must have felt something like that. Paul and Peter were dead, victims of an unreasoning persecution. First-generation Christians were in the clutch of advancing years. For many, the blessed hope of the Savior's return had become tarnished with delay and disappointment. Defection was common. The little Christian community was at sea. They needed the kind of assurance that this little story radiates.

Mark was the first to write it. Later Matthew wrote his version of it, remembering what (apparently) Peter had rather forgot: the lapse of faith on the water. And when John wrote his Gospel, much later than either of the others, this precious, hope-giving, heart-warming story became one of his seven signs.

The story itself speaks of at least three things: (1) strange demand; (2) sympathetic Savior; and (3) secret strength. May we look at them in some detail?

Strange Demand

Mark tells us that Jesus made his disciples get into the boat, and without him. We understand from the story why Jesus did this. Each of the gospelists agree that there was some rash talk running through the crowds; talk of revolt, of independence, of armed uprisings. Jesus did not want his disciples infected with that virus. He made them put out to sea. He isolated them from the crowd.

Sometimes we find ourselves isolated from our own crowd by our Christian service responsibilities. Assume responsibility for a Sunday School class, a Church Training group, a youth organization. And if you take it seriously at all, you soon find yourself cut off. Your friends are free to go and come as they like. They have no responsibilities. But you are under the strange demand.

Others may lie in on Sunday morning, but you cannot. There are those who would be disappointed were you to do that. Others may take Sunday afternoon and evening for their own enjoyment, but you must not. There will be faces—some turned toward you in eagerness, some turned away in apathy—to confront, and hearts to challenge. You are under this strange demand. Jesus is still putting his honest-to-goodness disciples in little boats, sending them out on the sea of Christian service and responsibility. It is his strange demand.

There are other times when sickness isolates us from the crowds, from our usual haunts. We get in the boat of illness, and set out on a sea of suffering. We, who were so independent and self-reliant, are left flat on our backs with not enough strength to turn ourselves in bed. This is the moment when we can understand the perplexity that troubled the disciples—why this strange demand? What had they done? In the sterile loneliness of a hospital room, where the only language is a tear, what means this strange demand?

Like the disciples, we will come to understand the loving purpose in the demand. But for now, such a demand can be met only in trust and faith. Age has a way of teaching us that lesson. Youth can only assume its truth. More than thirty years ago, as a young preacher, I lived beside two wonderful Christian widows. One was a Roman Catholic; the other a Methodist. Both had drunk deep of the chalice of grief, trouble, and sorrow. And one day, the little Roman Catholic widow handed me a poem that I have kept through all these years. It was a veteran's prayer for a young, unmarked soldier under the strange demands of the Savior.

Yours be the hope that falters not through sorrow,
   But keeps its flame still burning clear and bright;
The hope that looks ahead to each tomorrow,
   And sheds its steady glow into the night.

Yours be the knowledge and the sweet assurance
   That comes to those whose faith is deep and true;
Yours be the heart that's trusting and courageous
   Through every day that lies ahead of you.

If you find yourself under the strange demand, be comforted. This sign points to that demand as the way of our Savior with his own.

Sympathetic Savior

But there is more to this sign than simply the demand we are under. The sign points beyond itself to a sympathetic Savior. He is sympathetic because he is man. His own necessity for prayer is the evidence. All the gospelists agree: Jesus withdrew to pray. And he is Savior because he is God. That is the meaning of his coming on the water.

Much of the New Testament is better understood if we have firm grasp of the Old. And in the Old Testament—where God is revealed in the wonders of nature—a favorite means of picturing the power of God is in reference to the sea. When God wanted to deliver his people, he parted the sea. Even the lively sea could not swallow Jonah in the story of the prophet. You see, God was preserving him. One of the psalms has a graphic passage about God and the sea, the mere reading of which will throw light on our sign. It goes like this:

> They that go down to the sea in ships, that do business in great waters; these see the works of the Lord and his wonders in the deep. For he commandeth and raiseth the stormy wind, which lifteth up the waves thereof. They mount up to the heaven, they go down again to the depths: their soul is melted because of trouble. They reel to and fro, and stagger like a drunken man, and are at their wits' end. Then they cry unto the Lord in their trouble, and he bringeth them out of their distresses. He maketh the storm a calm, so that the waves thereof are still. Then are they glad because they be quiet; so he bringeth them unto their desired haven (Ps. 107:23–30, KJV.)

Steeped as they were in the images of the Old Testament, the apostles came to understand the meaning of Jesus' coming to them on the water. The message was so startling as to be scarcely believable—Jesus was Lord of nature. They came to understand Jesus' walking on the water as a sign. He came to them in the "fourth watch of the night"—that darkest part of the night, just before the dawn—but any good friend might do that. It was that he came to them as Savior!

Richard Watson Gilder, American poet and editor, had some lines that have been quoted often:

> If Jesus Christ is a man—
> And only man—I say

That of all mankind I cleave to him
  And to him will cleave alway.

If Jesus Christ is a god—
  And the only God—I swear
I will follow Him through heaven and hell
  The earth, the sea, the air.

About those lines the famous Presbyterian preacher, Dr. Clarence Macartney, once wrote: "The last part (of that verse) is sense and reason; the first part is nonsense. If Jesus Christ be man, and only man, there is nothing in him worth following and worth cleaving to. The poet sings as if it made little difference which way the vote fell—man, or Son of God. But it does make a difference—an immeasurable difference." [2]

The difference is that between a sympathetic friend and a sympathetic Savior. Jesus came as Lord of nature and with power to help.

Secret Strength

Though John does not record this detail in his reporting of the sign, Matthew gives us the human story of Peter, setting out with buoyant enthusiasm to walk to Jesus on the water, only to become fearful and sink in white-capped waves. When Peter's attention fastened on the wind and the waves rather than the Savior, he began to sink.

It is strange, isn't it, how what has your attention has you? If you meet life in faith, you can figuratively walk on the water. But if you are fearful and anxious, then life's billows threaten and you begin to sink in a sea of anxiety.

When I was a boy, we used to play a game called "walking the plank." We started out with the plank on the ground, and almost everyone could walk it. But after each turn, the plank was elevated a little higher from the ground. First it was cement blocks; then saw-horses; finally step-ladders. And every time the plank went a little higher, some of the walkers were eliminated. Why? The plank was still as wide as ever—as wide as when it was on the ground. What eliminated us one by one was the fact that we began concentrating on the space around the plank rather than on the plank itself.

Sometimes our prayers do more damage than good. We fill our minds with our needs, rather than with the power and willingness of the Savior to meet our needs. We concentrate on our weakness instead of his strength. We fill our thoughts with our problems rather than his power. We look at ourselves when we should be looking at our Savior.

But Peter recovered himself. As he sank he cried, "Lord, save me." That is a good prayer. It is a prayer we need to pray. Some of us need to pray that prayer as Christians. Some reader may need to pray that prayer for salvation, for the new and eternal life that is in Christ Jesus. All of us need to pray that prayer, whatever the sea we sail, for it is only the Savior who can save us.

St. Francis of Sales noticed that in the country area where he lived servant girls, when drawing water from the wells, would place a piece of wood in the brimming pail. He was told, upon inquiring the reason for the practice, that the wood kept the water steady.

So, when we are distressed and agitated by life's events, we must keep Christ and his cross at life's center. That will steady us. That is the secret of peace, whatever sea we must sail. Life is fraught with hazard, hurt, and risk. Our fund of courage could soon be spent. But if Jesus is in the midst of our lives, if we fasten our hearts to his, then we sail the seas of life in peace. And at the last, we come into the harbor with eternal joy.

12 What Do You See?
John 9:1–8; 19–21, 24–29

The American sculptor, Lorado Taft, once described a summer vacation he enjoyed with his family on a northern lake. Each day they hurried through the evening meal so they could watch the sunset. One evening their maid asked to bring her parents to watch the sunset with the Tafts. Mr. Taft agreed, but commented that her father and mother had seen hundreds of sunsets. The maid replied that they had never seen a sunset until the Tafts came.[1]

Imagine that: People who never saw a sunset until others made them aware. They had missed the splendor all around them. That, in a far more profound sense, is what John is saying in this sixth sign. Speaking for those who had come to see life through the eyes of Christ, John seems to be saying that they had been living in the opaque shadows, a kind of eerie half-light, until Jesus came. You cannot read the story without sensing that it points beyond itself. Following his usual style, John comes on in two wavelengths. It is the story of a man who came to see the light of day, but it is also the story of a man who came to see him who is "the light that lightens every man" as well.

The format of the story is drama. One way of getting into the drama is to ask, What did the principals of the story see? And that is my question. We shall ask what some of the crowd saw; what the parents saw; and—at the last—what the blind man himself saw. And as we ask these questions we are aware that we shall find ourselves, our own capacity for seeing, somewhere among these principals.

What the Crowd Saw

The *neighbors and friends* indicate what they saw with their question, "Is not this the beggar?" (v. 8). This was not a matter of condescension, it was identification. Once a beggar, always a beggar. They were convinced that a leopard never changes his spots. (See Jer. 13:23.) So they had him labelled—"a beggar."

Not that they did not have a shadow of guilt pass over them concerning the man. Often they had seen him out begging for alms. It was his only livelihood. He was dependent upon the charity of others. And as he sat on the corner, or at the gate to the Temple, they felt in passing a slight twinge of irritation, even anger. But always they passed on with a shrug and a comment, "Oh, that's our beggar."

Don't be too hard on those neighbors. We have probably all done the same. We have some neat stereotypes we put people into, like slots in a file: alcoholic, loafer, hippy, no-good, bum. And somehow just to classify them eases our conscience.

Did you notice that Jesus came on this man just outside the Temple? Isn't that ironic? The one who most needed what the Temple represented never got inside. Nor, apparently, was his darkness relieved by so much as the warmly human, sympathetic touch of a mitered priest. Is it any different now? Is it not true that the ones who most need the church are often not found within it? They are just on the outside, perhaps even at the gate. But they do not come in, not as often as we should like. Perhaps they cannot. At least they feel they cannot. Like the beggar, they have little to encourage them.

The *neighbors* saw a beggar.

The *apostles* disclosed what they saw by their question: "Who sinned, this man or his parents, that he was born blind?" (v. 2, RSV). They saw a theological problem. The mere sight of the blind man was enough to launch them into a ponderous discussion of hackneyed old theological themes which professional religionists had been gnawing at for a thousand years.

I read somewhere of the bonsai trees in Japan. They are malformed over as much as four hundred years. A young pine is set in one inch of soil in a shallow dish. As the tree grows, each root is trimmed and the branches cut back. The tree is tended so for nineteen or twenty generations, and it never outgrows this shallow dish. So the bonsai tree becomes a patriarch, standing twenty inches high, very much alive, with a gnarled and twisted top three feet across. Well, the disciples had come on a theological bonsai tree. They were going to get the answer from the oracle himself. So when they saw the blind man, they saw an old, contorted, theological problem: "Who sinned, this man or his father, that he was born blind?"

It is easier to ask a question like that than to grapple with the flesh-and-blood problem.

The *neighbors* saw a beggar. The *apostles* saw a theological problem. But *Jesus* saw a man: "As he passed by, he saw a man" (v. 1, RSV).

Jacob Riis, as a young newspaper reporter in the late nineteenth century, made a visit to the ghetto section of New York City, and what he saw drew him back again and again. Finally he wrote a book about the kind of life some men live, victimized as they are by ignorance, superstition, poverty, and their own apathy. He titled his book *How the*

Other Half Lives. Theodore Roosevelt, among the first to read the book, was deeply moved by it. He went to see Mr. Riis at his office, but the author was out. Thereupon Mr. Roosevelt took out his calling card and wrote that he had read the book and had come to help.

We would be mistaken if we were to conclude that theology is unimportant. But our mistake is only compounded when we let theology become more important than helping people. For theology was never meant to be anything more than an engine—it supplies the motive power for practical service.

If you were to ask who has better theology, the professor of a seminary handing out little theological *bon-mots*, or the layman in city hall grappling with the problems of law enforcement and sociological blight, I would have to cast my ballot for the layman. Theological professors are necessary, but when Jesus passed by, he saw a man. And I might add, a man for whom he would soon die.

So that is part of the drama: what the neighbors, the apostles, and our Savior saw.

What the Parents Saw

As this little drama unfolds, the parents are called before an investigating committee of the Pharisees. It is not that the Pharisees are conducting an unbiased inquiry. They have already reached a verdict. They are simply looking for supporting evidence. They are going at their business as some people go to the Bible. It is not that they want to let the Bible speak to them; they want to speak to the Bible. Theirs is not an openhearted search for truth. Why should it be? They already have it! All they want is corroborating evidence, a prooftext of some kind. Even the devil is good at finding odds and ends of Scripture lying around that can be used to advantage. You may recall how he kept spouting Scripture to our Lord in the wilderness temptation: "It is written, He will give his angels charge concerning thee, lest haply thou dash thy foot against a stone." (See Luke 4:10–11, quoting Ps. 91:11.)

So this is a time-honored tactic, and the Pharisees are honoring their progenitor by its employment.

The first question is heavy with innuendo: "Is this your son, who ye say was born blind? [As though they would lie about a thing like that!] How then does he now see?" (v. 19).

And in that question the parents saw trouble coming. They answered cautiously, but honestly. The first part of their answer was emotion-laden: "We know that this is our son, and that he was born blind" (v. 20, RSV).

They could remember the joyful preparation for that child. It was a tender time. They discussed the question of a name. If a boy, then it would be named after the father, or by his choice. If a girl, it would be named after the mother, or by her choice. They had rejoiced in the child's coming. They remembered his first stirrings in the mother's womb, and remembering, these plain, honest, uncomplicated people replied, "This is our son."

But they went on, and in that continuation was the pathos of a lifelong disappointment: "And he was born blind." There had come that awful time when they confirmed their son's blindness. He could not see. Not a thing! But they loved him. They arranged the furniture in the house for easy passage. They taught their son every door, every chair, every table. All through the years that mother never changed a piece of furniture. She put the food on the table in clock-wise fashion, and taught her son how to find it. In spite of their disappointment, they loved their son, and in their homespun way had done the best by him they possibly could. They admitted the emotion-laden obvious: "We know that this is our son, and that he was born blind."

But that was as far as they could go. Beyond that admission was the threat of excommunication. And they were old; too old they thought to break out of their own religious security system. If we are not careful, age will make us timid. Middle age is that perplexing time of life when we hear two voices. One is the voice of our youth asking, Why not? The other is the voice of our years asking, Why bother? The parents of the story had come to that place where they were guided by that last question: Why bother?

Perhaps you are of advancing years. Through all these years you have set a certain pattern, a style for your life. You have never included in that style an open avowal of Jesus Christ as your Savior. And you observe that you have made it thus far with no more distress than the next. Why bother with this baptism and church membership bit now? Well, why not? Your reading of these lines is an admission that you are drawn to the things of Christ. Why not openly avow him? Is it timidity? is it fear that keeps you from it?

What do you see in the Savior? Only a problem? That is all the parents of the blind man saw, and noble as they were, in this they failed. They said, "How he now sees we do not know, nor do we know who opened his eyes. Ask him; he is of age, he will speak for himself" (v. 21, RSV).

What the Blind Man Saw

And that brings us to the blind man. What did he see?

Well, of course, he saw the light of day. But that was only the beginning. He came to see Jesus as the Light of the world. And that process is worth examination. How does one come—in the spiritual sense—from darkness to light?

It begins, it seems to me, in an openness to truth.

The adequacy of any truth may be determined by the number of significant facts it explains. The Pharisees' truth had one troubling fact it could not explain—how the blind man had come to have sight.

On the face of it, Jesus was the explanation. But the Pharisees were blind to the possibility that God could come to men in ways outside their institutional forms. This ruled Jesus out. He stood outside the pale. He was neither priest nor scribe. He had to be a charlatan.

But the blind man saw the inadequacy of their truth, and remarked upon it:

> Why, this is a marvel! You do not know where he comes from, and yet he opened my eyes. We know that God does not listen to sinners, but if any one is a worshiper of God and does his will, God listens to him. Never since the world began has it been heard that any one opened the eyes of a man born blind. If this man were not from God, he could do nothing (vv. 30–33, RSV).

How adequate is the truth you have been living by? Does it give you power for the present and hope for the future? How open are you to new truth? to new demands the gospel lays upon us in light of changing circumstances? A long time ago a very wise man wrote:

> God offers to every mind its choice between the truth and repose. Take which you please—you can never have both. . . . He in whom the love of repose dominates . . . gets rest, commodity and reputation; but he shuts the door to truth. He in whom the love of truth predominates . . . will abstain from dogmatism. . . . He submits to the inconvenience of suspense and of imperfect opinion, but he is a candidate for truth, as the other is not, and respects the high law of his being.[2]

The blind man saw a new truth, and at whatever risk, he embraced it. But the blind man did more than embrace abstract truth; he embraced him who is true: Jesus the Lord.

As the curtain falls on the drama, John reported Jesus as

saying to the entire cast—Pharisees, parents, neighbors, apostles, blind man: "My coming into this world is itself a judgment—those who cannot see have their eyes opened and those who think they can see become blind" (9:39, Phillips).

Jesus requires a certain humility of us. He goes before leading us into new meanings and new demands, all flowing from his inexhaustible truth. We are under judgment. The judgment is cast in the molds of just what it is we see. And whatever else we may see, this we must see: Jesus Christ towers above all our man-made institutions and forms. He judges them in terms of how well or how poorly they express his concern for the last, the least, and the lowly; of how well or how poorly they get across the idea that he makes every man, woman, and child a unit of infinite worth.

13 Lazarus Laughed
John 11:38–44; 12:9–11

Jesus had discretely departed Jerusalem after his controversy with the Jews. Although the tides of time were running out swiftly, Jesus was concentrating on his present task—the further training of the men upon whom would fall the responsibility of carrying on his mission. His sense of urgency was accentuated by the brevity of his time—just about three months, and then Golgotha.[1]

In the midst of this training program, done on the field as Jesus met human need, an emergency message came from Bethany. Lazarus, his beloved friend, and the brother of Mary and Martha who had so often befriended him and his disciples with the hospitality of their home, was seriously ill. Death threatened, and the sisters had asked Jesus to come.

A significant commentary on the means of God's providence lies in the fact that Jesus did not go immediately. His ways have not changed. Often when we ask something from God we discover that God is not as hurried as we are. Divine providence sometimes moves slowly. But it always carries an unsuspected blessing.

When, after two days had passed, Jesus shared his purpose of going to Bethany (just two miles from Jerusalem), his disciples were deeply disturbed. They knew only too well the danger that such a trip involved. Thomas, to whom we do not customarily attribute decisiveness, finally suggested to the other disciples, "Let us also go, that we may die with him" (11:16).

At that point Jesus intimated that they were on the threshold of the most startling experience they had ever witnessed. His purpose, he let them know, was to do more than go to Bethany. He intended to invade death's domain and there snatch from death his stranglehold on the hearts of men.

The understanding of the disciples may have been hazy, but none can gainsay their devotion. They were accompanied to Bethany by serious misgivings, but that did not deter them. Their courage was equal to their fears.

Once in Bethany, some four days after the emergency message had first arrived, the disciples soon caught a glimmer of Jesus' intent. Lazarus was dead. Jesus had been conducted to the graveside, in company with Jews from Jerusalem, the sisters Martha and Mary, and his disciples. Once there, Jesus had commanded the stone rolled away from the tomb. After a simple prayer of thanksgiving, Jesus cried out in a clear, loud voice, "Lazarus, come forth!"

The Bible is eloquently concise in the way it tells the story. Nothing is mentioned of the look of incredulity that must have passed over the faces of some; nor the sense of dark horror that must have possessed the sisters, one of whom had protested earlier that the body was in a state of decomposition; nor of the wide-eyed wonder of Mary when Lazarus actually emerged from the tomb. None were prepared for that; they were all frozen in fear and wonder. Jesus was compelled to command the obvious, "Unbind him, and let him go!"

Three Imagined Episodes

Not long after this point in the story Jesus retired to a

little village called Ephraim. Lazarus and his sisters returned to their home in Bethany. And a group hostile to Jesus reported this strange happening to the chief priest in Jerusalem. He added it as one more particular in his bill of indictment against Jesus.

When next we meet Lazarus, it is a few days before the crucifixion. Lazarus and his sisters were hosts to Jesus. The Jews journeyed out from Jerusalem, not only to see Jesus, but also to see Lazarus—this man whom Jesus had raised. And while the common people were satisfying their curiosity, their leaders came to a decision: Not only must Jesus die, but Lazarus must die also!

But that is the conclusion of these events. What might have happened in those intervening weeks—those days between Lazarus' raising and this final brutal decision on death to them both? If imagination can be trusted, then let us follow it to the inner chamber of the high priest of those days. Could he have reasoned thus? "If I can get Lazarus to publicly state that all this was a hoax, that he was never really dead, I can cut the ground out from under this peasant prophet. Now, what could I offer Lazarus that might induce him to such an admission?"

A few days after that scene, see another. There comes to the home of Lazarus a high official of the chief priest's office. After the courtesies have been exchanged, the official says, "Lazarus, we know that this raising-from-the-dead business is a fraud. If you will make suitable public statements to that effect, I am prepared to secure you a seat on the Sanhedrin for the rest of your natural life."

Now the Sanhedrin, for any devout Jew, was a body of splendor and honor. It entitled him and the members of his family to a high position in the society of Jerusalem. To be one of the seventy rulers of Israel? Ah, that was an honor some men spent the most of a lifetime to attain.

And what did Lazarus do? Lazarus laughed. Beginning with a low chuckle, which seemed to mock this pompous official who knew nothing of the real values of life, Lazarus' laugh swelled into a rolling, musical denunciation of the entire scheme. Humiliated and nonplussed, the chief priest's messenger retired in confusion.

Several days passed. Then, early one morning a prominent Jerusalem businessman stood knocking on the door to Lazarus' home. Though Lazarus did not know it, this businessman was financially obligated to Caiaphas, the chief priest. He was just one more caught in the web of Caiaphas' entanglements. The businessman had a proposition which was fabulous. "Lazarus," he said, "I am prepared to make you a full partner in my business. As you may or may not know, I have trade throughout the Roman Empire. I have branch offices in Athens, Alexandria, and Rome. Your income, conservatively, would be enough in one year to provide for a comfortable retirement. Only one condition is attached. You must denounce, publicly, this Jesus. You must announce that your recent, ah, er—publicity stunt, was a hoax. You do that, and you will never have another financial worry for all of your natural life!"

Lazarus looked about slowly, and caught the poor man's eye. As the flower wilts in the heat of the sun, so the bravado of this businessman melted before the insistent but compassionate gaze of Lazarus. The man felt as though he were naked. Suddenly, he was unaccountably ashamed.

And then, slowly and softly at first, Lazarus began to laugh. As a parent will sometimes laugh at his child who is caught in a transparent fraud, so Lazarus laughed at this unmasked, hollow man. Without a word, the man of business rose to his feet and was gone.

Still following imagination's muse, we see a third scene. It is the week of the crucifixion, and Jesus is now guest in Lazarus' home. This third visitor from Caiaphas is less subtle. Gone is the courtesy, the deference. This time it is a soldier. Imperiously, he has intruded on the privacy of Lazarus' home, forcing his own entry. "I have come, Lazarus," he announces, "to warn you. If within the next twenty-four hours, you do not confess your fraud in the matter of your little graveside drama with Jesus of Nazareth, Caiaphas, the chief priest, will have you before the Sanhedrin. You will be tried by that body, condemned, and delivered to the Romans for execution."

The soldier watched Lazarus intently as he spoke. He was looking for some sign of weakness, of fear. But none came. Lazarus looked on the soldier much as a father would look at his blustering four-year-old who was ordering him to his execution. A moment passed, and in that moment, it was the soldier who was afraid. And then Lazarus, who had come back from death and was now threatened with death, began to laugh. His laughter was slow, compassionate, and compelling. It was a knowing laugh; a laugh directed not at the soldier, but at old death. Lazarus had been delivered from the fear of death.

Three Christian Realities

Admittedly, these episodes are pure imagination. We have no biblical record to support them. But we do have this: every sign in John's Gospel was written with a purpose beyond the telling of a lovely story. Perhaps our imaginary vignettes are true to John's purpose in this story—to underscore the fact that the Christian, like Lazarus, has been delivered from the thralldoms of this world. We are new creatures in Christ Jesus. We do now, through the Spirit, participate in the divine life. Death, pride, and the desires of this world have lost their power.

Three significant realities, which ought to possess everyone of us as Christians, emerge from this sign. The first reality is in the possession of an eternal treasure. Matthew 13:44 identifies as treasure the kingdom of heaven. In the Matthew passage, the value of the treasure surpassed all others, and was possessed by the sacrifice of all else. In Matthew, that treasure is God's eternal kingdom, and the gospel of Jesus Christ opens to us its door.

In 2 Corinthians 4:7 Paul identified the Christian's treasure as "the light of the knowledge of the glory of God in the face of Jesus Christ." The point of Paul's summation is that God has done something remarkably unique in Jesus Christ; he has brought his own glory down close to men. And when a person has known the splendor of God's glory, what lesser glory can compare? Jesus Christ delivers us from every lesser master.

Is that not what happened to Lazarus in our imagined episodes?

The second reality which emerges from Lazarus' sign is that of a wonderful friendship. He has Jesus for a friend. That friendship explains Lazarus' loyalty to Jesus, even in the face of dire threat. (See John 12:9–11.) For you see, in one sense at least, we are what our friends make us.

Do you know the story of Dürer's famous painting, "Praying Hands"? Dürer was born in Nuremberg, Germany, the son of a Hungarian goldsmith. Because he was one of a large family, Dürer lacked the money to do what he most wanted, to study art. Eventually his father allowed him to leave home to study with one of the great artists of the day. But because Dürer had to make his own way, his life as art student was a desperate struggle. Finally, he found an older friend who also wanted to be an artist. They decided to live and study together. Dürer offered to be the first to work while the other studied.

However, his older friend objected: "I am older. I have a place to work in the restaurant, and I do not have so much talent. I will work and you will study." So the older friend washed dishes, scrubbed floors, and spent long hours at menial labor while Albrecht Dürer developed his artistic skill.

Eventually, Dürer sold a wood carving. He came home with the money and said to his older friend, "Now, it is your turn." The older friend took up his brush and his paints and enrolled for study. But the hard work had stiffened his muscles, enlarged his joints, and gnarled his fingers until he was unable to wield the brush with the required delicacy and skill. Reluctantly, he gave up his dream of painting.

Dürer grieved that his own skill had come at the cost of his friend's. Then one day, Dürer saw those work-worn hands folded in prayer. In that moment he found inspiration for the painting we know and love. "Praying Hands" was Dürer's tribute to a friend whose sacrifice made possible his skilled art.[2]

In the raising of Lazarus, the gospelist John culminated his witness to the human Jesus.[3] The fact that Jesus knew he risked death to go to Lazarus, and went anyway, speaks of the quality of his friendship. But many of us have run risks because we were friends. Is there more? Yes, there is more. As the God-man, the friend Jesus broke death's grip on Lazarus, his friend. Lazarus was free because his friend Jesus had made him so. Is that not true of every person in Christ? If not, it ought to be.

A final Christian reality drawn from this account is the

freedom from fear which should characterize every Christian. Do you recall how in each of the three imagined episodes Lazarus met a bribe or a threat with laughter? Perhaps you asked as you read along, What is the writer's meaning? Why these imagined events, each ending with Lazarus' laughter?

My meaning is this: through Lazarus' experience of death and raising he had learned the poverty of those values by which the world teaches us to live. Those values do not last. Power, wealth, even length of days have no eternal significance.

Moreover, Lazarus learned to live life to the full. No longer did he trim his sails before the fear of death, or the promise of gratifications that can never satisfy. The world's tyranny over Lazarus was broken.

We have said that John wrote as an apologist and an evangelist. In recounting the story of Lazarus, John was expounding the meaning of Jesus' promise: "I came that they may have life, and have it abundantly" (John 10:10, RSV). Lazarus' sign says that Christ frees us from every crippling fear.

14 King for a Day
John 11:55 to 12:19

The Feast of the Passover [1] in the first-century Jewish world was, as we said in chapter 5, something like our Christmas. It celebrated the deliverance from Egypt, and so marked Israel's redemption from bondage. Passover was more than holiday; it was holy day. At Passover families gathered in remembrance of that wondrous night when they were delivered by God's hand under Moses. Incorporated in Passover observance was the Day of Atonement and the annual sacrifice for the people's sin. Passover was heavy with religious significance.

Passover, as we said earlier, was also something like our Fourth of July. It marked the real beginnings of Israel as a nation. At this season all the ancient national aspirations of Israel burned at white heat. Israel expected at some Passover or Tabernacles to be greeted by a new Moses. He would make the street grafitti, "Roman go home!" an accomplished fact.

The Feast of the Passover in A.D. 29 was no exception. Jews poured into Jerusalem from the four points of the compass. Faces flushed with excitement, spirits bright with anticipation, they crowded the streets and public places of the city. It was what the newspaper commentators would have called an explosive situation. And there was tinder enough in Jerusalem to explode it. Word of the raising of Lazarus over in Bethany—just two miles from

Jerusalem—had excited the wildest kind of messianic hopes. The name Jesus was on nearly everybody's lips. The question asked was, Is Jesus our new Moses?

Hope for the Messiah had worn thin in the past four hundred years. It had been that long since God had spoken by one of his prophets. Since then the Seleucids had overrun their land. Judas Maccabees and his brethren had jolted the messianic dream for a brief moment about two centuries past. But they had soon fallen to quarreling among themselves and the thread of political and military power had come unravelled. The Romans had come and set their oppressive heel down hard upon the people. Since then Israel had been restive under the alien Herods, whose ancestry traced back to the hated Edom. But now, there was this Jesus. It had been too long since Israel had heard a voice lifted in their land, crying, "Thus saith the Lord!"

Of course, there had been John the Baptizer. But he had come to nought. One of the Herods, Antipas, had dispatched him at Machaerus. He had fanned the flames of messianic hope, but briefly. The nearest thing to a divine intervention had been those Maccabees. They had given Judea a taste of political freedom, and it had whetted the appetite. The brief splendor of that era, like an incandescent beam which rises in stark splendor on the horizon, had risen to fan the hopes of many a patriot. But midway in flight it had sputtered out, leaving the political night all the darker. It had served—that era—to give the Judeans a glimpse of what might be. Judea was hungry for hint of a Messiah.

Such was the explosive situation. It explains the spontaneous reception given Jesus as he entered the city on the day we have come to call Palm Sunday. In a word, the Jews thought they had found their Messiah. They believed they were witnessing the dawn of the day of deliverance from the oppressor. The era spoken of by the prophets had come. Jesus, son of David, was king of the Jews!

The quiet irony in the story (and we do know how it turns out) lies in the fact that before the week was over this crowd and others had led Jesus outside that city to be crucified. Jesus was acclaimed king on Palm Sunday, true. But he was only king for a day.

However, the story and its truths cannot be told that easily. The currents lie deep, but they are discernible. Let us look at them in this fashion: (1) a need for authority; (2) false authorities; and (3) the One having authority.

A Need for Authority

We begin with a simple statement. Most people want an authority over them. In Shakespeare's *King Lear*, a lesser nobleman comes to Lear and says, "You have that in your countenance which I fain would call master."

"What's that?" asks Lear.

"Authority," answers the nobleman.[2]

Early in the Bible we find this need for authority emerging. The Israelites came to Samuel and said, "We would have a king." Old Samuel wept his eyes red, for he knew what a king would mean to this people. Their hard-won freedom would be lost to a king, a man like themselves. And there were overtones of Samuel's own grief at what he took as rejection. God comforted his champion by reinterpreting the direction of the request: "They have not rejected you, but they have rejected me from being king over them" (1 Sam. 8:7). And to meet Israel's desire for a king Samuel anointed Saul to be king over Israel.

It seems that every nation accommodates itself to this deep need to live under some kind of authority. The names differ, the function does not. The authority may be called prince, or prime minister, or queen, or king, or president, or emperor. But somewhere in the social compact of human arrangement you will find an authority figure. It is a deep-seated need.

Taking the idea a step farther, every culture has some kind of religious authority figure. For the Hindu it is Brahma. And there are others—Confuscius, Muhammad, Moses, Zoroaster, Buddha, and so on. For the Christian, there is Christ. Man seems to have deep within him an unrest with things as they are. He lives on the latent hope that some authority will rise out of the masses and lead him from the morass of confusion and ambiguity he knows into a promised land of security and self-realization. The politician's promise is directed toward this need; that is why he is dangerous, and his promise to be received with skepticism.

Well, the Jews of Jesus' day were human beings. They had had Moses, and were looking for another like him. Jesus seemed to fill the bill. He excited in men, as the Gospels record, this deference to authority. Early on, you will recall, Matthew told how "the crowds were astonished at his teaching, for he taught them as one who had authority, and not as their scribes" (Matt. 7:28–29).

As you scan the pages of the Gospels you find the names of men and women who responded to Jesus like that. Zacchaeus, you will recall, climbed a sycamore tree so that he could better see Jesus. The Samaritan woman, hopelessly involved in a life of personal ruin, talked with Jesus about this common hope: "We know that Messiah is coming."

Nicodemus, powerful, socially prominent, found himself irresistibly drawn to Jesus. His first recorded word of conversation is a subtle acknowledgment of a recognized authority resident in Jesus.

Blind Bartimaeus, having heard of Jesus' coming, could not contain his own excitement about Jesus. Although he could not see him, he could cry out to him: "Have mercy upon me, thou Son of David!" And the Jews, John's Gospel tells us, having heard about the raising of Lazarus as the last of a series of awe-inspiring deeds, were standing on tiptoe in their excitement about Jesus. Perhaps all the old promises were true!

I recall hearing Dr. Duke McCall tell in his inimitable way of an experience he had during World War II. At that time he was living in New Orleans and preaching for Dr. George Truett at the First Baptist Church of Dallas.

Dr. Truett was smitten with the illness that finally took him, and Dr. McCall was making the trip by train each weekend. On the particular occasion of which he told he was riding opposite two young women and two soldiers. The two young women were doing their best to get the attention of the soldiers, and the soldiers were preoccupied with their own efforts to make an impression on the young women. It is funny, you know. When boys are small all they care about is soldiers in uniform, and when girls are small all they care about is painted dolls. But give them a few years, and all the girls care about is boys in uniforms and all the boys care about is painted dolls. I guess that's a trick nature plays on us all.

So, the young people opposite Dr. McCall were mutually flirtatious. Meanwhile, the porter came into the car and began making up the berths. Dr. McCall had his books spread all about, keeping them handy for his sermon preparation for the next day. The porter saw that he was busy and skipped his berth. The people across the aisle were not quite so fortunate, and the young ladies asked Dr. McCall if they could sit on the yet unmade seats of his berth. He gathered up his books, put them away, and tried to be gracious to the young ladies. They sat down opposite him and began to practice their wiles on him.

"What do you do, mister?" one of them asked.

Dr. McCall assumed a brassy air and replied, "I preach the gospel!"

"Oh, that old stuff!" came the reply.

"Yes," said Dr. McCall. "That old stuff." And then not quite knowing why he went on, "Wouldn't it be wonderful if it were true?" Beginning at that point he talked for a long time to the young ladies about their spiritual need.

The next morning, as they were preparing to leave the train, Dr. McCall found himself at one end of the car, the platinum blonde and her companion at the other. The blonde caught a glimpse of Dr. McCall and had soon edged her way through the car to where they could continue the conversation of the night before. "What's the matter, young lady?" asked Dr. McCall. "Were you thinking about our conversation of last night?"

"Dr. McCall," she said, and a tear began to trickle down her cheek, streaking her artificially tanned face, "I couldn't sleep last night for thinking how wonderful it would be if God really cared for me." We need not be afraid that a word about Jesus will be inappropriate. He is God's response to man's need for authority.

False Authorities

Most persons have an innate need for an authority, we have said. But we must add to that statement this other: Most persons want an authority subject to their manipulations. The Jews wanted a king, but they wanted a king who would do as they wanted. This double-edged need tempts both ways. It tempts those persons who want an authority to withhold commitment until the person wanting to be authority conforms to the wishes of those he seeks to lead. At the same time the would-be authority is tempted to submit to the demands made in order to become the authority figure. Let's see how that principle worked in Jerusalem.

The throngs of Jerusalem knew the kind of king they wanted. The first step was to whet his appetite. "Hosannah," they cried. That cry meant, "Save now!" and its meaning is a clue to the crowd's goal. They would use Jesus to attain their own ends. And to use him they would first flatter him. They knew what they wanted, and they thought they knew how to get it.

But Jesus knew that although they knew what they wanted they did not know what they really needed. They thought they needed a king while they really needed a Savior. Is that not like us all—to confuse felt and real needs? This confusion between felt and real needs results in a confusion about goals and the means to attain them. So Plato wrote about an ideal republic and dreamed himself to be the ideal philosopher king. But his contemporaries never took him or his republic seriously. The gap between the ideal and the real was too great.

Seneca, that bright apostle of the Stoic philosophy who lived in Nero's era, praised the poverty of his contemporaries while he revelled in his own luxurious surroundings. If the goal was happiness and the means to attain it was asceticism, why did the philosopher sell his soul for the trappings of wealth and power? He stooped so low as to fraudulently write the shameful document by which Nero defended the murder of his own mother.[3] Seneca thought he knew what he wanted. As his tutor, Seneca had made his own master in the emperor Nero. But what Seneca wanted he did not really need. And what he needed he did not want. In the end he needed to be saved from the master he had made for himself. The emperor Nero ordered the aging philosopher to take his own life.

You may think you know what you want. You may talk about old-age security, having fun in the sun, raising a family to be proud of, and other good goals for a life. But what of this basic flaw? This tendency to confuse felt and real needs? This proclivity to adopt corrupting goals and then use corrupting means to attain them?

Jesus is God's way of meeting us at the point of our deepest real need. He resisted the crowd and their intention. When it came right down to the wire, Jesus was not their kind of king and he would not let himself become one. We must not try to make Jesus king after our own fashion. We must not try to tell God what we need and how those needs should be met. We must let God tell us what we need and show us how those needs can be met.

One of the differences between Jesus and ordinary men and women is that, given the opportunity, Jesus refused to play fast and loose with people's need for authority. Jesus would not be false to any man, even those who wanted to make him king.

One Having Authority

So the crowds met Jesus at St. Stephen's gate on that first day of the week long ago. They cried their "Hosannahs"; they strewed their palms in his way. They were ready to make him king.

I cannot help but wonder where those same people were on Friday. Some say Friday's crowd were different people, and they may have been. But where were the kingmakers? Why such fickle commitment?

When Jesus came from Bethany
To Jerusalem one day,
The throngs cried their "Hosannahs!"
Strowed palms along the way.

"Welcome to old David's son,
Long live our king!" they cried.
He was the hero of the hour,
Great was his fame, and wide.

But Jesus rode upon an ass—
No royal throne for him;
He wanted nothing but men's hearts;
No gold, no crown, no gem.

The throngs were not content for long,
And soon they changed their cry;
Within the week the cross was made,
They left him there to die.

The crowd's commitment was fickle because Jesus would not conform to their expectations. He needed no authority they might confer; he was authority. He "did not trust himself to them, because he knew all men and needed no one to bear witness of man; for he himself knew what was in man" (John 2:24–25).

So the crowd turned away, and some of them doubtless turned on him. Jesus had been their king for a day. He wanted to be their king for alway, but they would not let him. It is not different today.

But Jesus journeys on today,
His quest is yet the same—
He seeks not my "Hosannahs!" but
My life committed to his name.

He meets me as I travel on—
"Long live my king!" I cry;
But do I mingle with the crowd
And leave him there to die?

15 Breakthrough

John 1:14; 6:48; 8:12; 10:11; 11:25; 14:6

An elderly woman once said to me something like this: "Jesus is real. I can feel close to him. He lived a good life; he was warm, friendly, full of compassion and understanding. He speaks to me and I do my best to follow him. But God—that is something else again. He is remote; he sometimes seems as cold as a star to me. I cannot make him out at all."

Her complaint about God and his impenetrable mystery is not unique. Long ago Blaise Pascal set down similar thoughts in his *Pensées:*

> I look around in every direction and all I see is darkness. Nature has nothing to offer me that does not give rise to doubt and anxiety. If I saw no sign there of a Divinity I should decide on a negative solution: if I saw signs of a Creator everywhere I should peacefully settle down in the faith. But seeing too much to deny and not enough to affirm, I am in a pitiful state, where I have wished a hundred times over that, if there is a God supporting nature, she should unequivocally proclaim him, and that, if the signs in nature are deceptive, they should be completely erased; that nature should say all or nothing so that I could see what course I ought to follow.[1]

God's mystery is couched quietly in the stories of the Old Testament, too. In fact, the story about how the Jews got their covenant name for God, which illustrates this facet of the Bible's revelation, leaves as much untold as told. You may recall the story. Moses had encountered the burning bush and heard the commanding Voice. In an effort to get his credentials in order for the mindboggling task assigned him, Moses asked a very sensible question: "If I come to the people of Israel and say to them, 'The God of your fathers has sent me to you,' and they ask me, 'What is his name?' what shall I say to them?"

Now notice the response. "God said to Moses, 'I AM WHO I AM.' " (See Ex. 3:14–15.) Other translations of God's response to Moses appear in small type in the Bible I am using as I write, but the gist of all the translations is that the name given by God to himself has at its core an impenetrable mystery. Actually, interpretations of God's name run from the idea of God's assertion of his being in every man's now to the idea of God's promise of adequacy for every man's future need. Paul Tillich's "ground of being" idea about God was drawn from this name for God. But whatever the interpretation, the assertion God makes about himself stands, I AM. And that assertion became the Jews' covenant name for God—Yahweh.[2] The name did not relieve, but rather heightened the element of mystery, however; the Jews refused to pronounce that covenant name and in its stead voiced the word *Adoniah*. Thus they verbally perpetuated the mystery which God's very name suggests.

Now all of this—the elderly woman's honest confession to her pastor, Pascal's plea, and the account of Moses' encounter with the Hebrews' God—sustain the fact of God's mystery. And to that fact the gospelist John addressed himself in his Gospel. Early on he wrote, "The *Logos* was God . . . The *Logos* became flesh." By his use of the word *logos* John set out the dramatic idea that a breakthrough had occurred; God's mystery had been unveiled. In John's time the word *logos* was used to express the idea that every animate form had the power to manifest itself. God also has this power, John implied, and he exercised it in a man called Jesus of Nazareth. Jesus was God concretized.

This idea is implemented in John's Gospel by a quiet bit of subtle artistry which we could easily overlook. John took the divine name, I AM, and in a series of predicates set out various facets of God's self-disclosure in Jesus. Thus we have the following statements falling from the lips of Jesus (RSV):

"I AM the bread of life" (6:48).
"I AM the light of the world" (8:12).
"I AM the good shepherd" (10:11).
"I AM the resurrection and the life" (11:25).
"I AM the way" (14:6).

This way of using the divine name was John's way of saying that a breakthrough into God's mystery has happened. In Jesus of Nazareth, and in a variety of modes, God has made himself known. His medium of self-disclosure was human life—"The Word became flesh." His message of self-disclosure was closely linked with human need.

Perhaps we can see more clearly the linkage of medium and message to life and need by pausing to set out a test by which we can gauge the accuracy of a truth, any truth. That test is this: *How well does this truth correspond to the real facts of human experience?* Each of the I AM statements makes a claim about the validity of God's relating to human life and need. If we can identify the human need linked with each I AM statement, then we can test its validity. We will know, from our own experience, whether or not it relates to life. With that in mind, we look at each of them.

"I AM the bread of life."

Prior to this statement Jesus had responded to the

people's physical hunger with bread. Having discovered in Jesus a ready source of that which sustains physical life, the people were ready to make a swap—their political support of Jesus for his power to make them secure; their freedom for his bread. But Jesus would have none of it. He spirited himself away, only to appear later to the disciples as they cowered before a storm on Galilee.

However the crowds would not be faked off that easy. Fired by a pious expectation that a new Moses would appear with the power to provide bread,[3] they pursued Jesus to Capernaum and pressed their claim. In response Jesus reminded them that when the people ate the first Moses' bread it did not make them secure; they nonetheless died in the natural course of events. And then Jesus made the claim, "I AM the bread *of life*" (author's italics).

What did Jesus mean? How does that statement relate to life? Perhaps Viktor Frankl, who spent seven years of World War II in Nazi concentration camps at Auschwitz and Dachau, can help us answer such questions. Out of his experiences in the crimped kind of life lived in concentration camps Dr. Frankl came to see that in life the question, Why? is more basic than either of the questions How? or What? As inmate of these horror chambers Frankl noted that some persons shriveled and died while others managed to survive. When he applied the observation skills of his psychiatric training to the problem, he concluded that the difference lay in a sense of meaning; a sense of purpose. He wrote of his findings, "The 'mode' of life—that is, its characteristic hardships and ennuis—retreats to the background the moment that, and to the extent that, the reasons for life come to the fore."[4] In other words, security may be a *felt* need, but meaning is a *real* need. When people had a sense of meaning for their lives they could withstand the insecurities of a prison camp and survive. And in the best of circumstances a life without meaning tends to flatten.

Now Jesus' statement about the bread of life roots in this real need of humankind, this need for meaning. With God as the center of a life, any life becomes bearable. That is the sense of Matthew Arnold's poem about the impoverished minister who was nourished inwardly by the bread of life:

"Twas August, and the fierce sun overhead
Smote on the squalid streets of Bethnal Green,
And the pale weaver, through his windows seen
In Spitalfields, look'd thrice dispirited.

I met a preacher there I knew, and said:
"Ill and o'erwork'd, how fare you in this scene?"
"Bravely!" said he; "for I of late have been
Much cheer'd with thoughts of Christ, the living bread." [5]

Jesus' statement avers that God meets us at the point of our real need, the need for meaning in life.

"I AM the light of the world."

Tabernacles, the Jewish feast of harvest, featured a ceremony which may have served as backdrop for this second statement. Raymond E. Brown writes of that ritual: "On the first night (and perhaps other nights as well) there was a ritual of lighting four golden candlesticks in the Court of the Women. . . . In the Gospel scene Jesus stands in this same Court of the Women and proclaimed that he is the light, not only of Jerusalem, but of the whole world." [6] That is the statement. How does it relate to the reality of human experience?

One of light's characteristics is its power to illuminate darkness. That fact may be a clue. Let me illustrate. Lord Salisbury, a British political leader, expressed fears for the post-World-War-II world during that crisis of civilization which have come to pass with an almost uncanny accuracy. This is what he said:

> More than death, wounds and destruction I dread the moral desert that lies ahead. . . . This war is going to destroy the moral sense of nations. Values that it has taken generations to establish will be smashed. I do not mean the political and economic changes that are bound to come. They may be good for us all. I cannot say. But the smashing of absolute standards of morality that you and I believe in, the denial of truths of the spirit, the elevation of man's mind and body in place of God—these are things out of which nothing but darkness and decay can come, and these are the things that I see before us.[7]

These thirty-six years later our dismal statistics on broken homes, rampant venereal disease, increasing numbers of illegitimate children, growing pre- and extra-marital sex, political venality on the national and international scene and much more stand as mute proof of Salisbury's foreboding vision. Without judgment on the merits of that war or its opposing forces, few would deny that mankind turned from the light given them in its prosecution. Perhaps the latest trends on the national and international scene forecast a turning back toward the light. Whatever the case, God is the touchstone of human morality. He is the light, even as Jesus declared him to be, and revealed him to be in his own life and teaching. Without God's light man descends to the darkness of the jungle.

"I AM the good shepherd."

We usually read John 10:1–21 in isolation from its setting. That's not our fault; if we must fix blame, let's place it on Robert Stephanus who made the chapter divisions in our Bibles way back in 1553. Actually, the material in which this statement comes belongs right along with the whole Tabernacles' scene, beginning at 7:10 and ending at 10:21. The immediate background is 9:41 which sets out

Jesus' harsh indictment of Jerusalem's religious leaders. In this statement we have a contrast. In essence, Jesus was saying, "While you can't trust them, you can trust me and the God who sent me."

For evidence of the truth of that claim John set right in the middle of the passage the story of how Jesus gave sight to a blind man. You may recall that sign. While the religious leaders put the blind man out of religion's pale, Jesus met his need and took him to himself.

The challenge of churches and churchmen today is to carry out this commitment Jesus made for himself and his followers. No one has seriously challenged Jesus' own commitment to the ideal. If a credibility gap exists in today's world, it is with Jesus' followers, not him. That was Maxwell Anderson's message in his play *The Wingless Victory*. The play was set in Salem, Massachusetts. Nathaniel had been away a long time, but had returned with a Malay princess as his wife. She had been attracted to what she had been told about Jesus, his teachings, his way of life.

But the people in Salem were narrow, mean, and prejudiced. They would not accept her. The pressure was so great that her husband weakened and sent her away with the children. She boarded the ship resolved to die, and in that dark hour she turned back to the pagan gods she had known in her childhood. She talked to them about this Christ whom her husband's people professed to follow and to whom she had been drawn. She spoke of her belief that he (Christ) had come too soon; that the world might be ready to receive him in a hundred thousand years, but not now.

In that poignant play Anderson was saying, "Christ and the God whom he came to make known you may be able to trust, but not his followers." John the gospelist made one point, and only one: Christ reveals a God you can trust. That truth corresponds to human need.

"I AM the resurrection and the life."

Death is real enough, and the lives lived in fear of it are real enough, too. Longfellow remarked on that in his poem "A Psalm of Life":

> Art is long, and Time is fleeting,
> And our hearts, though stout and brave,
> Still, like muffled drums, are beating
> Funeral marches to the grave.

What of Jesus' statement on this very real human need?

Well, in the first place Jesus gave the sign of Lazarus' raising. That sign shook Jerusalem's religious leaders. In fact, it precipitated Jesus' own rendevous with death. His subsequent triumph over death we celebrate every Easter. But how does that series of events relate to me? you ask. This is how, if you are a person of Christian faith: "You were buried with him in baptism, in whom also you were raised through faith in the energizing of God who raised him (that is, Jesus) out of the dead" (Col. 2:11, author's translation).

But resurrection life in the here and now is not all of it; beyond is the resurrection hope. The New Testament teaches the resurrection of the body (see 1 Cor. 15). Because of Jesus' bold statement and authenticating triumph, the cemetery is transformed from a graveyard to a garden. For the fear of death he gives hope; for death he offers life. This truth meets human experience at a point of real need.

"I AM the way."

Plato is supposed to have prayed for a god, or a god-inspired man, who would show men their duty and how to live as they ought. John's proposition is that God has sent such a man in Jesus of Nazareth. But more than that, God has manifested himself in Jesus. In that self-disclosure Jesus linked areas of real human need with God's provision for each need. He did so through many media, one of which is the linking of the divine name, I AM, with real and universal human needs. Is John's proposition true?

I affirm that it is. God meets me at the point of need in my own experience. He gives my life meaning; he has proven trustworthy; he illuminates my understanding; he has given me hope for life and beyond. He is the way for me.

John wrote as an evangelist who believed Jesus did bring men to God and eternal life. "These things are written," he wrote, "that you may believe that Jesus is the Christ, the Son of God, and that believing you may have life in his name." That which John wrote has the ring of reality to it, at least for me. Christ's claims match my needs. Do they yours?

I learned to drive an automobile on a *Model T.* Perhaps that is the reason I remember this story from many years ago. A proud owner of a *Model T* was stranded with his car in the open country. It would not run, and he did not know how to make it run. While pondering his problem another motorist in a large Lincoln automobile stopped. After asking permission, the second motorist began tinkering with the *Model T* and had it running in no time. When the first motorist tried to pay for the help, the good Samaritan refused. In an embarrassed effort to make transitional conversation, the *Model T* owner remarked, "You certainly do know how to make one of these cars go." And the tall man replied as he turned to his own car, "I ought to. I invented that car. My name is Henry Ford."

John's message is that God knows how to help us where

we hurt because he made us, and because he chose to become one of us. John's Gospel is commentary on one inspired sentence written by the apostle Paul: "God was in Christ, reconciling the world unto himself." That breakthrough is gospel.

Notes

Chapter 1

1. From *The New Testament in Modern English*. © J. B. Phillips, 1966. Used with permission of the Macmillan Company. All succeeding quotations are marked (Phillips), and are used by permission.
2. "Communist Exploitation of Religion," Hearing before the Subcommittee to Investigate the Administration of the Internal Security Act and other Internal Security Laws of the Committee on the Judiciary, United States Senate, Eighty-ninth Congress, Second Session. Testimony of the Rev. Richard Wurmbrand, May 6, 1966, p. 24. U.S. Government Printing Office, Washington D.C. 20402.
3. *Ibid.*

Chapter 2

1. Bob Merrill (lyrics) and Jule Styne (music), "People," from *Funny Girl*.
2. In the RSV translation of John 1:41 the word *first* is placed in the sentence so as to suggest immediacy. However, based on early texts, a proper rendition could be, "Andrew found his own brother Simon first." Read that way, the meaning is that Andrew found Simon before John found James. This reading makes possible the location of Simon's call in Galilee, as is done by each of the Synoptic Gospelists. (See Mark 1:14–18; Matt. 4:18–20; Luke 5:1–11.) The assumption here is that Simon's call came in Galilee.
3. As told to the author by Charles Trentham, pastor, First Baptist Church, Washington, D.C.
4. Edgar J. Goodspeed, *The Twelve* (Philadelphia: John C. Winston Co., 1957), p. 33.

Chapter 3

1. G. Avery Lee, *Life's Everyday Questions* (Nashville: Broadman, 1953), p. 66.
2. Walt Whitman, *Leaves of Grass* (New York: Grosset & Dunlap), p. 359.

Chapter 4

1. Elizabeth B. Browning, "Aurora Leigh."
2. Joseph Mary Plunkett, "I See His Blood Upon the Rose," in James Dalton Morrison, *Masterpieces of Religious Verse* (New York: Harper & Brothers, 1948),

p. 201.
3. B. B. McKinney, "What Will You Do with Jesus?" *The Broadman Hymnal* (Nashville: Broadman Press, 1940), p. 101.

Chapter 9

1. Wilma Dykeman, *Prophet of Plenty, The First Ninety Years of W. D. Weatherford* (Knoxville: The University of Tennessee Press, 1966), p. 87.
2. From Norman Vincent Peale, "The Wonderful Thing About People," in privately published sermon dated October 23, 1966, and identified as Volume 18, no. 3.

Chapter 10

1. This poem was given to the author by Dr. Charles Trentham, then pastor of First Baptist Church, Knoxville, Tennessee. Original source unknown.

Chapter 11

1. Joseph Conrad, "Typhoon," *Portable Conrad* (New York: Doubleday & Co., Inc., 1955), p. 207. Reprinted by permission of J. M. Dent & Sons, Ltd. London.
2. Clarence Macartney, *Macartney's Illustrations* (New York: Abingdon Press, 1946), p. 49.

Chapter 12

1. Robert Hastings, *A Word Fitly Spoken*, (Nashville: Broadman Press, 1962), p. 54.
2. Ralph Waldo Emerson, *Essays, First Series: Intellect*, as cited in Burton Stevenson, *The Home Book of Quotations* (New York: Dodd, Mead & Company, 1964), p. 2055.

Chapter 13

1. John 10:22 mentions the Feast of Dedication which falls in our December. John 12:1 mentions Passover (our Easter). The interim between John 10:22 and 12:1 had to be about three months.

2. Lawrence P. Fitzgerald, "The Hands of Jesus," *Pulpit Digest*, March, 1965, p. 41.

3. In John 8:56 Jesus used the expression "my day" in reference to his entire ministry. Jesus' use of the word *day* in 11:9 indicates that he recognized that his ministry was about to come to its night, that is, to its close.

Chapter 14

1. Jewish feasts are prominent in John's Gospel. Jesus' first and last signs John placed near the Passover. The sign of the wine at the wedding in Galilee followed a Passover; the sign of Lazarus' raising in Bethany preceeded a Passover. In between, John placed Jesus in Jerusalem at the time of two other prominent Jewish feasts—probably Pentecost and certainly Tabernacles. (The feast of 5:1 was probably Pentecost, which comes fifty days after our Easter. John 7:2 identifies the Feast of Tabernacles as the occasion of the events in John 8—9. The time of Tabernacles is early winter—close to our Thanksgiving. John 12:1 identifies

Passover as the season in which Lazarus' raising occurred, as well as those subsequent events which culminated in Jesus' crucifixion.)

The Jewish feasts served John as a means for interpreting Jewish expectations—such as the coming of Messiah during the Feast of Tabernacles—as fulfilled in Jesus. They provide a framework for John's theological interpretation of Jesus. The Passover Feast setting of John 12:1 and following presents Jesus as the ultimate paschal lamb offered for all time for the sins of all people. (See Heb. 9:15–28.)

2. Shakespeare, *Twenty-Three Plays and Sonnets* (Chicago: Charles Scribner's Sons, 1938), "King Lear," Act I, Scene 4, 11. 29–32.

3. See Will Durant, *The Story of Civilization, Caesar and Christ* (New York: Simon and Schuster, 1944), pp. 277,301–307.

Chapter 15

1. Blaise Pascal, *Pensées* (Baltimore, Maryland 21207, 7110 Ambassador Court: Penguin Books, Inc. © A. J. Krailsheimer, 1966), pp. 162–63.

2. The American Revised Standard Version translated the Hebrew consonants "Jehovah." However modern scholarship tends toward the soft pronunciation of the consonants, hence, "Yahweh."

3. The *Apocalypse of Baruch* has this sentence with respect to the expectation of a second Moses: "It shall come to pass at that self-same time that the treasury of manna shall again descend from on high, and they will eat of it in those years because these are they who have come to the consummation of time." See Raymond E. Brown, *The Gospel According to John I-XII* (Garden City, New York: Doubleday & Company, Inc., 1966), p. 53.

4. Dr. Viktor Frankl, "The Constant Quest for a Meaning to Existence," in *The National Observer*, Monday, July 12, 1965, p. 22.

5. Quoted in Barclay, *And He Had Compassion on Them* (Edinburgh: The Church of Scotland Youth Committee, 1955), p. 168.

6. Raymond E. Brown, *op. cit.*, p. 344.

7. Quoted by R. N. Usher-Wilson, "Fragmented Morality and the Social Drift," in *Christianity Today*, December 17, 1965, p. 15.